113th U.S. OPEN
Merion Golf Club

Written by David Shedloski Photography by the USGA Edited by Bev Norwood

ISBN 13: 978-1-878843-69-2
ISBN 10: 1-878843-69-9

©2013 United States Golf Association®
Golf House, Far Hills, N.J. 07931

Statistics produced by IBM

Course illustration by Robin Moline

Published by IMG Worldwide Inc.,
1360 East Ninth Street, Cleveland, Ohio 44114

Designed and produced by Davis Design

Printed in the United States of America

Justin Rose's solid victory in the U.S. Open Championship at Merion came as no real surprise to me. I was certainly aware that he had been playing very well the past few years. Then he verified that for me in March when he played very well and came close to winning my Arnold Palmer Invitational Presented by MasterCard, finishing a close second to Tiger Woods.

He was very much in command of his game throughout the week and proved himself at Merion, especially as he held off Phil Mickelson and the other challengers in Sunday's tight finish on Merion's strong closing holes. The outcome had to be particularly disappointing for Phil, as yet another strong bid slipped through his fingers over the final holes.

I thought Merion itself was also a winner that June weekend. Questions had been raised when the United States Golf Association announced its return to the classic Philadelphia course after a 32-year lapse. Was it too short for today's players? Would they overpower it and produce record low scores, embarrassing Merion and the USGA?

I never really thought so. I felt sure that length would have nothing to do with the difficulty of Merion. It played extremely tough, demanding skillful, strategic shotmaking, not big tee shots, and proved itself as a great test of U.S. Open Championship golf. The biggest problem Merion faced was accommodating all of the extra facilities that go with major championships within the narrow confines of the club's property and the surrounding residential neighborhood. It seemed that they came up with some unique solutions in that regard and made it all work.

This is the 29th edition of this annual publication produced by Rolex, a great corporate friend of golf, presenting this most recent U.S. Open in wonderful words and pictures for its readers. I'm sure you will enjoy it.

Arnold Palmer

The 16th hole, par 4 and 430 yards.

113th U.S. OPEN
Merion Golf Club

The mystique of Merion Golf Club begins with its iconic wicker baskets. The manifestation of that mystique could be found in the perplexed players who walked off Merion's venerable and viably enervating East Course during the 113th U.S. Open Championship awed by its antithetical identity: small but pugnacious; seemingly benign yet eminently burdensome; amenable to prudence while provoking impertinence.

Easy to be hard.

Or, as William Flynn, the original Merion greenkeeper who over time had a major influence on Hugh Wilson's brilliant design, summed up: "Apparent simplicity, actual complexity."

Though 32 years removed from the last time it hosted American golf's national championship, Merion, it was discovered, hadn't lost its charm or its innate challenges. True, recent upgrades and a stretching of some key holes awakened the fabled East Course from its antediluvian slumber. But the authentic essence of the layout was left intact, and it was its innate intractable nature that was put to the test June 13-16, 2013, against a new century of championship golfers — men of immense physical talents, big, fit, well-coached and wielding high-tech implements — who were programmed to rend asunder classic examinations such as Merion in a grossly anachronistic mismatch.

But over the four days of the championship — four days that brought rain and sun and varying winds and universal puzzlement — it became obvious that few people really knew Merion, even if they could say they were aware of how intricately Merion is woven into the fabric of American golf history. Just as St. Andrews, in Scotland, is considered the home of golf, many aficionados have taken to calling Merion the home of American golf, even though it was not the first club in the new world. This proud distinction Merion has earned through its timeless architectural rendering and through a history of championship golf played upon it that yielded winners of almost sacred renown: Bob Jones, Ben Hogan, Jack Nicklaus, Lee Trevino.

Tucked along the leafy Main Line 11 miles west of Philadelphia in Ardmore, Pa., Merion Golf Club draws its origins from a long ago time and from another recreational pursuit: cricket.

Fifteen men from Lower Merion Township, led by Haverford College students William Montgomery and Marshall Ewing, founded the Merion Cricket Club in 1865 with the express purpose of meeting once a week to play. But by 1879, more members had become interested in tennis, and barely a decade later golf started to make inroads into the psyches of the athletically minded American citizen.

Records show that on November 20, 1895, the Merion Cricket Club formed a committee to explore introducing golf to the members. Soon thereafter, plans were made to build a nine-hole course on a farm in Haverford Township. The first five holes were completed in May 1896, and the remaining four in the fall, all at a cost of roughly $600. More than 150 members joined to play golf, and within a few years Merion Cricket Club's golf membership had doubled to nearly 300. It was obvious that the nine-hole course had become insufficient to handle demand.

An additional nine holes were completed in 1900,

but within a decade, with improvements in equipment — particularly the introduction of the rubber-cored ball — the Haverford course clearly had become obsolete, and another committee was formed that voted to seek a piece of property to build a new 18-hole course. The committee, which included an enthusiastic and highly skilled amateur golfer named Hugh Irvine Wilson, eventually selected a 120-acre tract south of the Philadelphia and Western Railroad tracks on both sides of Ardmore Avenue, not far from the existing club. Just months later, another 6 acres were added to the L-shaped property that possessed dramatic, flowing topography.

Wilson, who had been captain of the Princeton golf team, seemed like a natural choice to design the course. After all, he had even ventured to Scotland and England to study the architecture of the famous old courses there and brought back with him many fine ideas that he infused into the layout. Or so the story goes in the 1989 book on the club's history. But that is folklore.

Club records show Wilson never missed a golf committee meeting in 1910 and 1911. He did venture abroad in 1912 — after he'd completed laying out the new 18-hole course, one with winding fairways, interspersed blind shots and green complexes of varying size and perplexing slopes. A British newspaper confirmed Wilson's presence in a report about an American golfer from Haverford inspecting the country's courses. Wilson so thoroughly enjoyed the exercise that he remained a month longer than scheduled and canceled his passage for return on April 10, 1912, on the White Star Line's newest, safest and most opulent passenger ship — the *H.M.S. Titanic*.

When Wilson returned, he and Flynn set about adding around 100 bunkers to the course. The rough-hewn, irregularly shaped, deep-faced bunkers, some later decorated with Scotch broom, came to be known as the "white faces of Merion," and their placement elevated the strategic brilliance of the layout to incomparable levels.

On September 12, 1912, the old course at Haverford was officially closed, but with the completion of the West Course in 1914, Merion became the first 36-hole golf club in the country. On September 14, the new course, then called the Ardmore Course, was opened. A newspaper report of the opening said the course was considered "among experts, the finest inland links in the country."

Richard S. Tufts, who served as president of the USGA in 1956-57 said Merion was a "model test of golfing skill and judgment for future architects to copy."

Legendary instructor and collegiate coach Eddie Merrins, the famed "Little Pro," who began his career by serving as an assistant professional at Merion from 1957-60, said he knows of two prominent golf course architects who often visited Merion simply to walk the East Course. "Dick Wilson and Robert Trent Jones would be out there all the time, just taking notes, getting ideas," Merrins said.

Through the years, Merion Golf Club, which split from the Cricket Club in 1941, has earned accolades far and wide, perhaps none more momentous than from Jack Nicklaus, who said of the East Course, "Acre for acre, it may be the best test of golf in the world."

It's no wonder that, counting the two U.S. Women's Amateur championships held on the old Haverford course, Merion has hosted 18 USGA national championships, more than any other course. Oakmont (eight), Baltusrol (seven) and Oakland Hills Country Club (six) have hosted more U.S. Opens than Merion, but the mere fact that the compact course was given an opportunity for a fifth U.S. Open so long after it had hosted its last in 1981 is a testament to its transcendence as a championship examination.

Merion's long absence from the national championship rotation could be blamed on its shrinking footprint in relation to the growth of the U.S. Open and the lengths to which players today hit the golf ball.

When David Graham picked apart Merion with a brilliant closing 67 and 7-under 273 total in the 1981 U.S. Open, one shy of the 72-hole championship record at the time, there was a feeling among the players and USGA officials that Merion had lost its relevance as a supreme golf examination. Concurrently, the popularity of the championship demanded that it be held at venues of sprawling capacity necessary to house greater levels of corporate hospitality and other spectator amenities.

But the USGA had never given up on Merion, and when the course, after slight upgrades, held its own in the 2005 U.S. Amateur, the USGA knew that the East Course remained a viable U.S. Open layout, and Mer-

The ninth hole, par 3 and 236 yards.

ion was awarded the championship the following year.

"I think that while Merion may be short on the scorecard ... it absolutely has stood the test of time," said USGA Executive Director Mike Davis. "In fact, if you ask me to rank other U.S. Open courses against it, I would say Merion has stood the test of time in terms of going from hickories to steel-shafted clubs to the modern golf ball and so on. I think this place has stood the test of time maybe as good as anyone."

Still, there was a bit more work to be done. Merion measured just 6,544 yards for the 1981 championship. With pushing, pulling and prodding, Merion was brought to 6,996 yards, the first U.S. Open course to play less than 7,000 yards since Shinnecock Hills Country Club in 2004.

Throw in an assortment of enhancements and Merion East was more than adequately fortified to withstand whatever leading-edge assaults the field could fashion. And the idea that the players would have to hit shots with clubs similar to what players of the past had to create came to fruition.

As Pete Dye, the wily golf course architect, said, "Merion isn't great because history was made there. History was made there because Merion is great."

And what history there has been.

Simply stated, few golf courses in America possess the championship pedigree of Merion, which hosted its first USGA championship in 1904 when Georgianna Bishop defeated E.F. Sanford, 5 and 3, in the U.S. Women's Amateur at the Haverford course. Five years later, again at Haverford, Dorothy Campbell defeated Nonna Barlow, 3 and 2, in the 15th U.S. Women's Amateur.

The year 1916 brought 160 players to the East Course at Merion for its first national championship, the U.S. Amateur, and Charles "Chick" Evans Jr., made history when he defeated Robert Gardner, 4 and 3. The Indianapolis native became the first man to win the U.S. Open and U.S. Amateur in the same year, having triumphed in the U.S. Open three months earlier at the Minikahda Club in Minneapolis with a score of 2-under 286, which stood as the championship record for two decades.

That same championship also welcomed the debut of a 14-year-old "wonder boy" from Atlanta who reached the quarterfinals before losing at the hands of Gardner. That boy was Robert Tyre Jones Jr., who burst on the scene by shooting a handsome 74 on Merion's West Course in the first round of qualifying, one of the best scores of

The 11th hole, par 4 and 367 yards.

the championship. Before Gardner ended his run, Jones showed glimpses of his blossoming brilliance in the round of 16 when he defeated New Jersey standout Frank Dyer, 4 and 2, after losing five of the first six holes. In the first round, Jones had beaten 1906 U.S. Amateur winner Eben Byers.

Eight years later, after having won the 1923 U.S. Open at Inwood Country Club in New York, for his first national title and ending his "seven lean years" in championship golf, Jones broke through for his first U.S. Amateur at Merion, obliterating George Von Elm, 9 and 8, in the final. That victory started a remarkable run of five U.S. Amateur titles in seven years, the last of which came in 1930. The site, as fortune and fate would have it, was Merion, and the stakes could not have been greater.

Jones arrived in Ardmore having won the first three legs of what was, in that era, golf's four major championships — the U.S. Open, the British Open, the U.S. Amateur and the British Amateur. The pressure on Jones was stifling, but so was his golf in that magical year, and on September 27, Jones closed out Eugene Homans, 8 and 7, and completed the Grand Slam. Behind the 11th hole tee box, where Jones played his last official competitive hole, there is a plaque set on a rock to commemorate Jones' feat. It reads: "On September 27, 1930 and on this hole Robert Tyre Jones Jr. completed his 'Grand Slam' by winning the U.S. Amateur Championship."

In his autobiography, Jones acknowledged his special feelings for Merion, writing, "I could not have picked a more propitious setting for this final event of the most important golfing year of my life."

The U.S. Amateur would return to Merion four more times. In 1966, Gary Cowan defeated Deane Beman, future PGA Tour commissioner, in a playoff by one stroke after both shot 285, five over par, during an era (1965-72) when the Amateur was contested solely at stroke play. In 1989, South Carolina's Chris Patton defeated Danny Green, 3 and 1, in a championship that included the likes of future stars Phil Mickelson, Jim Furyk and Steve Stricker. And in 2005, Italy's Edoardo Molinari rallied from a three-hole deficit after 18 holes to defeat Californian Dillon Daugherty, 4 and 3.

American amateurs have thrived in team competitions at Merion. The USA Curtis Cup Team was victorious, 6-3, over Great Britain & Ireland in 1954, and in 2009 the USA Walker Cup Team was an easy winner over their GB&I counterparts, 16½ to 9½.

And then there was the 1960 World Amateur Team Championship at Merion, where the U.S. team defeated Australia by a massive 42 strokes, 834 to 876. Leading the way for the host Americans was Jack Nicklaus of Columbus, Ohio, who had won the 1959 U.S. Amateur at age 19 and earlier in the summer in 1960 had finished runner-up to Arnold Palmer in the U.S. Open, the best finish by an amateur since Johnny Goodman won the 1933 championship. The young Nicklaus was at the top of his game that week, shooting rounds of 66-67-68-68–269, regarded by golf aficionados as one of the most dominant performances the game had ever witnessed.

In 1934, Merion hosted its first U.S. Open and would welcome the national championship back in 1950, 1971 and 1981. Each proved monumental in its own way for the drama it produced and the quality of golf that was on display.

Olin Dutra won his only U.S. Open with a display of brilliant shotmaking and spirited determination as he overcame a severe stomach illness to defeat Gene Sarazen by one shot. Dutra, of Monterey, Calif., was briefly hospitalized before the championship and contemplated withdrawing after contracting food poisoning on the way to Merion. By the time the championship began, he already had lost 15 pounds, but he somehow persevered. Dutra trailed by eight shots after 36 holes, but rounds of 71 and 72, the former an impressive display in strong winds, made him the first native of California to win the U.S. Open. His comeback was the largest midway through the competition until Palmer matched it in his 1960 triumph at Cherry Hills.

Ben Hogan's victory in 1950 produced even greater storybook drama. Just 16 months after his near-fatal automobile accident, Hogan defeated Lloyd Mangrum and George Fazio in an 18-hole playoff, shooting 69 to 73 for Mangrum and 75 for Fazio. The final outcome of that Sunday seemed almost anti-climactic compared to what had unfolded the day before when competitors faced 36 holes.

Hogan, his legs weakened by the accident and in need of constant care throughout the remainder of his competitive career, had contemplated

The 18th hole, par 4 and 521 yards.

The 27 past champions attending dinner on Tuesday at Merion were (front row, left to right) Jack Fleck, Johnny Miller, Arnold Palmer, Lee Trevino, Curtis Strange, Tom Watson, Billy Casper, Lou Graham, and (back row) Lucas Glover, Michael Campbell, Angel Cabrera, Hubert Green, Rory McIlroy, Lee Janzen, Andy North,

withdrawing on the 13th hole of the second 18 that afternoon. Two holes earlier, on the famous 11th, he had struck a tee shot and then nearly collapsed, his aching knees nearly giving way as cramps settled into his thighs and calves. He just wasn't sure he could traverse the maze of hills at Merion, but somehow he trudged on, and received aid from playing partner Cary Middlecoff, who marked his ball on the greens over those final holes.

Still, Hogan three-putted the 12th and 15th and failed to get up and down from a greenside bunker at the par-3 17th to lose a three-shot lead. He needed a birdie at the 18th for the victory, a par to tie, and his 1-iron second shot into the green was one of the purest ever witnessed — or caught on film, as Hy Peskin captured Hogan, from behind, in his follow-through with what is regarded as a masterpiece of photography. Hogan got his par, two-putting from 40 feet, to finish at 287. The next afternoon, rested and revived, he claimed the second of four U.S. Open titles. A plaque in the 18th fairway marks the spot with these simple words: "June 10, 1950 U.S. Open, Fourth Round, Ben Hogan, 1-iron."

Jack Nicklaus returned to Merion in 1971 as the clear favorite for the 71st U.S. Open, and, sure enough, he finished first after 72 holes with a final-round 71 and even-par 280 total. Unfortunately for the Golden Bear, his friend and rival, Lee Trevino, had carded a 69 earlier and also was in at 280, setting up a playoff.

Trevino, who had won the 1968 U.S. Open at

113th U.S. Open

Tiger Woods, Webb Simpson, Tony Jacklin, Jim Furyk, Hale Irwin, Steve Jones, Jerry Pate, David Graham, Geoff Ogilvy, Raymond Floyd, Graeme McDowell, Tom Kite.

Oak Hill, was filled with confidence for that championship in no small part thanks to Nicklaus, who had pulled Trevino aside after the Merry Mex had skipped the Masters Tournament. Nicklaus had told Trevino he was good enough to win anywhere. Trevino proved him right with his 68-71 defeat of Nicklaus in the Monday playoff notable for the ice-breaking moment of humor before the first tee shot when Trevino pulled a rubber snake out of his bag. Even Nicklaus laughed at the gag, but his wedge game took a bite out of his chances as he twice failed to escape from greenside bunkers, giving Trevino a lead he never relinquished.

Before the playoff, a Wake Forest University golfer and Pennsylvania native named Jim Simons continued the tradition of amateur excellence at Merion by seizing the 54-hole lead with a scintillating 65. Simons eventually finished fifth, the best showing by an amateur since Nicklaus had placed fourth in 1961.

"Merion made my career," Trevino would say later, perhaps speaking not only for himself but also for so many others who had ever excelled on the East Course.

In 1981, David Graham's impeccable final round made him the first Australian to win the U.S. Open as he overcame a three-stroke deficit to George Burns on the final day. Graham missed only one fairway and he hit 15 greens in regulation and used his putter from just off the fringe at the other three in one of the great shot-making displays in the history of the championship.

"This place," Mike Davis summed up, "just from a historical standpoint and the great moments of golf … you can't find a better place."

11

Hideki Matsuyama was the only player to earn qualifying spots in both the 2013 U.S. Open and British Open.

Qualifying for the U.S. Open Championship is arguably among the most difficult tasks in all of sports. Just ask Zach Fischer, who went above and beyond the usual call to reach the 113th U.S. Open at Merion Golf Club.

Fischer, 23, a professional from Texarkana, Texas, needed 66 holes to qualify for his first U.S. Open, turning what is known as "Golf's Longest Day," which this time fell on Monday, June 3, into a golfing odyssey. Not only did Fischer survive an 18-hole local qualifier, but he then played in a 36-hole sectional at Lakewood Country Club in Dallas, where he tied for fourth with PGA Tour veteran Ryan Palmer.

The playoff that ensued for the final berth stretched into a second day and 12 holes before Fischer finally ended it with an 8-foot birdie putt.

"It was amazing. I've never been a part of anything like this," Fischer said. "You can't describe what it's like without being a part of it."

Even Palmer, 36, a fellow Texan who eventually got in the field as an alternate, agreed that it was special to be a part of such an epic contest. "This definitely goes down in the memory books," the four-time PGA Tour winner said.

Fischer had company in two-day playoff work. Florida club pro John Nieporte, 46, qualified for his first U.S. Open in his 19th attempt when he needed an extra day and a third playoff hole to beat 15-year-old Texan David Snyder in Bradenton, Fla.

Fischer and Nieporte were among the 80 qualifiers who joined 76 exempt players competing at Merion Golf Club's historic East Course.

Hideki Matsuyama, 21, of Japan, who turned professional in April, enjoyed the best championship among the qualifiers, finishing tied for 10th thanks to a closing 3-under 67, which equaled the lowest round of the week. Matsuyama had entered the championship on a roll, having won the sectional at Ohtone Country Club by four shots after winning twice and finishing second twice in his previous four starts on the Japan Tour.

"It was great to play here," Matsuyama said after his first U.S. Open. "It was a great experience for me to be able to play a course that was so difficult. To play well the final day has given me a lot of confidence and I'm looking forward to more experiences like this."

Ten amateurs, led by 2012 U.S. Amateur champion Steven Fox, made the field, marking the sixth time in the last seven years that amateur entrants cracked double digits. Seven of the 10 reached Merion via qualifying.

Including Fischer, 20 players advanced through both local and sectional qualifying. Another intriguing story was that of Canadian professional Mackenzie Hughes. At the local qualifier, he birdied the last three holes for an alternate spot, but then got a tee time at the sectional in St. Louis when Champions Tour player Jay Haas withdrew. A two-time Canadian Amateur champion, Hughes, 22, had to borrow money from friends and carry his own bag, but he birdied the last hole to get in a playoff, where he earned the last spot.

The USGA received a record 9,860 entries into the 113th U.S. Open, eclipsing the mark of 9,086 received for the 2009 championship at Bethpage State Park's Black Course. Qualifying was conducted at 111 local sites followed by 13 sectional qualifiers, two of them international.

13

Players Who Were Fully Exempt for the 2013 U.S. Open (76)

Keegan Bradley	7, 12, 13	Russell Henley	13	Ian Poulter	13
Angel Cabrera	1, 5, 13	Billy Horschel	13	Justin Rose	12, 13
Michael Campbell	1	John Huh	12	Charl Schwartzel	5, 13
Kevin Chappell	11	Freddie Jacobson	13	Adam Scott	5, 12, 13
K.J. Choi	8	Thongchai Jaidee	13	John Senden	11, 12
Stewart Cink	6	Dustin Johnson	12, 13	Marcel Siem	13
Tim Clark	13	Zach Johnson	12, 13	Webb Simpson	1, 11, 12, 13
Darren Clarke	6	Martin Kaymer	7, 13	Brandt Snedeker	12, 13
George Coetzee	13	Matt Kuchar	8, 12, 13	Kyle Stanley	14
Nicolas Colsaerts	13	Martin Laird	13	Henrik Stenson	13
Jason Day	13	Paul Lawrie	13	Kevin Streelman	13
Luke Donald	12, 13	Marc Leishman	13	Steve Stricker	12, 13
Jamie Donaldson	13	Hunter Mahan	12, 13	Michael Thompson	11, 13
Jason Dufner	11, 12, 13	Matteo Manassero	9, 13	David Toms	11
Ernie Els	6, 11, 12, 13	Graeme McDowell	1, 11, 13	Bo Van Pelt	12, 13
Gonzalo Fernandez-Castano	13	Rory McIlroy	1, 7, 12, 13	Nick Watney	12, 13
Rickie Fowler	12, 13	Phil Mickelson	5, 12, 13	Bubba Watson	5, 12, 13
*Steven Fox	2	Francesco Molinari	13	*Michael Weaver	2
Jim Furyk	1, 11, 12, 13	Ryan Moore	12, 13	Boo Weekley	13
Sergio Garcia	12, 13	Geoff Ogilvy	1	Lee Westwood	11, 12, 13
Robert Garrigus	12, 13	Thorbjorn Olesen	13	*Chris Williams	4
Lucas Glover	1	Louis Oosthuizen	6, 12, 13	Casey Wittenberg	11
Branden Grace	13	John Peterson	11	Tiger Woods	1, 8, 12, 13
Bill Haas	13	Carl Pettersson	12, 13	Y.E. Yang	7
Peter Hanson	13	Scott Piercy	12, 13		
Padraig Harrington	6, 7, 11	D.A. Points	13	*Amateur	

Key to Player Exemptions:

1. Winners of the U.S. Open Championship the last 10 years (2003-12).
2. Winner and runner-up of the 2012 U.S. Amateur Championship (must be an amateur).
3. Winner of the 2012 British Amateur Championship.
4. Winner of the 2012 Mark H. McCormack Medal (top-ranked in WAGR and must be an amateur).
5. Winners of the Masters Tournament the last five years (2009-2013).
6. Winners of the British Open Championship the last five years (2008-2012).
7. Winners of The PGA of America Championship the last five years (2008-2012).
8. Winners of The Players Championship the last three years (2011-2013).
9. Winner of the 2013 European Tour BMW PGA Championship.
10. Winner of the 2012 U.S. Senior Open Championship.
11. From the 2012 U.S. Open Championship, the 10 lowest scorers and anyone tying for 10th place.
12. Those players who qualified for the season-ending 2012 Tour Championship.
13. Top 60 point leaders and ties from the current Official World Golf Ranking as of May 27, 2013.
14. Top 60 point leaders and ties from the current Official World Golf Ranking as of June 10, 2013.
15. Special exemptions selected by the USGA.

113th U.S. Open

Sectional Qualifying Results

Ohtone Country Club - West Course
Ibaraki Prefecture, Japan
33 players for five spots

Hideki Matsuyama	67 - 65 – 132
*Jung-Gon Hwang	68 - 68 – 136
Yui Ueda	65 - 72 – 137
(P) Yoshinobu Tsukada	72 - 66 – 138
(P) Hiroyuki Fujita	68 - 70 – 138

Walton Heath Golf Club
Surrey, England
94 players for 12 spots

Simon Khan	67 - 70 – 137
Jaco Van Zyl	71 - 67 – 138
Paul Casey	74 - 64 – 138
Morten Orum Madsen	67 - 72 – 139
Peter Hedblom	67 - 73 – 140
Eddie Pepperell	70 - 70 – 140
Marcus Fraser	71 - 69 – 140
(P) John Parry	66 - 75 – 141
(P) David Howell	68 - 73 – 141
(P) Jose Maria Olazabal	68 - 73 – 141
(P) Estanislao Goya	69 - 72 – 141
(P) Chris Doak	71 - 70 – 141
(A) Rikard Karlberg	70 - 71 – 141

Big Canyon Country Club & Newport Beach Country Club
Newport Beach, Calif.
102 players for five spots

Bio Kim	62 - 71 – 133
Steven Alker	69 - 68 – 137
Roger Tambellini	69 - 68 – 137
(P) *Cory McElyea	69 - 69 – 138
(P) *Max Homa	66 - 72 – 138

Ritz-Carlton Members Golf Club
Bradenton, Fla.
56 players for three spots

*Kevin Phelan	65 - 70 – 135
John Hahn	65 - 71 – 136
(P) John Nieporte	71 - 66 – 137

Hawks Ridge Golf Club
Ball Ground, Ga.
51 players for three spots

Ryan Nelson	68 - 65 – 133
*Michael Kim	67 - 66 – 133
*Grayson Murray	69 - 66 – 135

Simon Khan

Jose Maria Olazabal

Kevin Sutherland

Qualifying

Charley Hoffman

Woodmont Country Club
Rockville, Md.
122 players for eight spots

Russell Knox	65 - 67 – 132
Randall Hutchison	65 - 67 – 132
Adam Hadwin	65 - 67 – 132
Ryan Sullivan	61 - 73 – 134
Matt Harmon	70 - 65 – 135
Cliff Kresge	66 - 69 – 135
Mathew Goggin	65 - 70 – 135
(P) Matt Bettencourt	70 - 66 – 136
(A) Harold Varner III	70 - 66 – 136

Old Warson Country Club
St. Louis, Mo.
42 players for two spots

Jay Don Blake	71 - 68 – 139
(P) Mackenzie Hughes	72 - 70 – 142

Jordan Spieth

Century Country Club & Old Oaks Country Club
Purchase, N.Y.
79 players for four spots

Jesse Smith	70 - 67 – 137
*Gavin Hall	70 - 67 – 137
Geoffrey Sisk	68 - 69 – 137
Jim Herman	70 - 68 – 138

Aaron Baddeley

Brookside Golf & Country Club & The Lakes Golf & Country Club
Columbus, Ohio
120 players for 15 spots

Charley Hoffman	65 - 68 – 133
David Hearn	69 - 65 – 134
Nicholas Thompson	68 - 66 – 134
Robert Karlsson	66 - 68 – 134
Josh Teater	63 - 71 – 134
David Lingmerth	70 - 65 – 135
Brandt Jobe	68 - 67 – 135
Brendan Steele	67 - 68 – 135
(P) Ted Potter Jr.	69 - 67 – 136
(P) Aaron Baddeley	67 - 69 – 136
(P) Luke Guthrie	67 - 69 – 136
(P) Rory Sabbatini	66 - 70 – 136
(P) Justin Hicks	66 - 70 – 136
(P) Sang-Moon Bae	64 - 72 – 136
(P) Doug LaBelle II	64 - 72 – 136
(A) Mike Weir	68 - 68 – 136

Springfield Country Club
Springfield, Ohio
39 players for two spots

Brian Stuard	65 - 64 – 129
Brandon Brown	70 - 65 – 135
(A) Ryan Yip	69 - 68 – 137

Colonial Country Club
Memphis, Tenn.
112 players for nine spots

Kevin Sutherland	66 - 67 – 133
Shawn Stefani	68 - 66 – 134
Jerry Kelly	67 - 67 – 134
Morgan Hoffmann	69 - 68 – 137
Joe Ogilvie	69 - 68 – 137
Scott Langley	71 - 67 – 138
Brandon Crick	70 - 68 – 138
(P) Alistair Presnell	71 - 68 – 139
(P) Andrew Svoboda	66 - 73 – 139
(A) Scott Stallings	70 - 69 – 139

Sang-Moon Bae

Shawn Stefani

Joe Ogilvie

Mackenzie Hughes

Lakewood Country Club
Dallas, Texas
68 players for four spots

Matt Weibring	70 - 64 – 134
Edward Loar	70 - 64 – 134
Jordan Spieth	67 - 67 – 134
(P) Zack Fischer	67 - 68 – 135
(A) Ryan Palmer	66 - 69 – 135

Tumble Creek Club
Cle Elum, Wash.
34 players for two spots

Wil Collins	70 - 68 – 138
*Cheng-Tsung Pan	69 - 70 – 139

*Denotes amateur
(P) Won playoff (A) Added to field as alternate

17

A tired-looking but satisfied Phil Mickelson (67) seized the first-round lead and the headlines.

113th U.S. OPEN
First Round

Phil Mickelson, who has a knack for making news as easily as he makes new fans, commanded the spotlight in the first round of the 113th U.S. Open Championship, his game soaring at the rain-softened but pugnacious Merion Golf Club despite the fact he'd barely had time for his feet to touch the ground.

Impressive and improbable was the 3-under-par 67 Mickelson submitted on Merion's storied East Course for the overnight lead, equaling his best start to the championship he covets most after finishing runner-up a record five times. Lefty's work was fairly airtight, four birdies against a lone bogey, after he had arrived at Merion a little more than an hour before his 7:11 a.m. tee time off No. 11 with good friends and U.S. compatriots Steve Stricker and Keegan Bradley.

"It was a very good start," Mickelson said of his opening salvo in his 23rd U.S. Open appearance, one that commenced with more putts at the first hole he played (three) than he had hours of sleep prior to teeing off (two). "You never know what's going to happen the week of the tournament, so you've got to prepare for all elements prior."

Few could ever predict what Mickelson is going to do the week of a championship, sometimes including Mickelson himself. This trait has endeared him to millions of fans around the world, but it has not always kept him entrenched at the top of leader boards.

But on this occasion, Mickelson's preparation was textbook — if Jack Nicklaus, always one of the most thoroughly prepared players in major championship history, wrote that textbook. From the outside it appeared that Mickelson had taken a most unconventional route to the first-round lead, and there was no denying that it had its elements of risk.

The 1990 U.S. Amateur champion, Mickelson had visited Merion the week prior before competing at the PGA Tour event in Memphis, the FedEx St. Jude Classic. He then showed up at Merion on Monday, but heavy rain showers since Friday had dumped more than 5 inches of rain on the compact East Course. Having planned all along to return to his home in Rancho Santa Fe, Calif., for the eighth-grade graduation of his oldest daughter, Amanda, Mickelson turned around and headed home where he could enjoy better practice weather.

Amanda and the U.S. Open are forever intertwined; she was born the day after the 1999 championship held at Pinehurst, in North Carolina. A 15-foot par save at the 72nd hole at Pinehurst's famed Course No. 2 gave the title to Payne Stewart by one stroke. Mickelson was there at the end, but all week he had carried a pager in his golf bag, prepared to withdraw if his wife, Amy, went into labor.

There was a "Circle of Life" quality to Mickelson's adventure as he circled over the continental U.S. while his peers were already fretting and fussing about the approaching examination. The graduation ceremony, at which Amanda gave a speech, began at 6 p.m. PDT. Mickelson boarded his private jet — clearly about the best way a father can use a private jet, too — at 8 p.m., and he was on the ground in Philadelphia at 3:30 a.m. He caught an hour's nap before arriving at the course, preferring to stay awake on his plane to review his notes on Merion, "relive the golf course," he said, and study

19

First Round

Bubba Watson (71) hit his first tee shot of the championship at the 11th hole.

First Round

Phil Mickelson	67	-3
Luke Donald	68	-2
Mathew Goggin	68	-2
Russell Knox	69	-1
Nicolas Colsaerts	69	-1

the green charts to get mentally prepared.

"Yeah, it might be abnormal, but it actually worked out really well," said Mickelson, who, coincidentally, shot 67 to begin the 1999 U.S. Open at Pinehurst. "I got all my work done on Merion when I was here a week and a half ago. I knew exactly how I wanted to play the golf course, given the conditions, given different wind conditions, clubs I was going to be hitting, where I was going to be, and the shots that I was going to have. So I didn't feel I needed more time at Merion, what I needed was to get my game sharp, to get my touch sharp. And having a nice practice facility and nice weather for the last couple of days allowed me to do that. So it worked out great on both ends."

It also worked out that Mickelson enjoyed a mid-round nap in the library of the clubhouse. Even Mother Nature seemed to have a soft spot for Phil and his quixotic quest.

Thunderstorms interrupted the competition

Luke Donald (68) gave two shots back after getting to four under par.

on two occasions, including a stoppage of three hours, 32 minutes less than two hours after Floridian Cliff Kresge struck the first shot of the championship at the No. 1 tee at 6:45 a.m. EDT. A second thunderstorm passed through at 6:10 p.m. for another delay of 45 minutes. Play was suspended for the day because of darkness at 8:16 p.m. with half the field, all 78 players from the afternoon wave, still on the course. When play resumed at 7:13 a.m. Friday, some men faced up to 32 holes. Good thing today's golfers are such devotees of fitness.

Second-round starting times were pushed back three hours.

England's Luke Donald actually went to sleep Thursday night with the dual identities of both leader and pursuer of Mickelson. He'd made birdies on his last three holes, including the short par-3 13th, to get to four under par, but that also meant Donald had the fearsome fivesome, holes 14-18, to

Russell Knox (69) played his final five holes in two under.

First Round

Mathew Goggin (68) as he watched a tee shot.

Lee Westwood (70) saved par from a bunker at the 15th.

Nicolas Colsaerts (69) shot an inward 32.

Charl Schwartzel (70) started steady.

complete. Sure enough, amid cold, damp conditions, Donald couldn't protect par along the closing stretch and finished at 2-under 68.

"Yeah, a complete switch in wind, and obviously a big drop in temperature. So those holes are playing long," said Donald, who was seeking his first win (and first top-10 finish, in fact) in his 10th U.S. Open appearance.

At least Donald stayed under par and in the hunt. Masters champion Adam Scott, playing with former U.S. Open winners Tiger Woods and Rory

113th U.S. Open

Masters champion Adam Scott (72) stumbled after the Friday restart to Round 1, losing five shots to par.

McIlroy in a pairing of the top three golfers in the Official World Golf Ranking, had a disastrous morning. The Aussie stood three under through 11 holes when play ended, but by the time he had holed out at the 18th, he had dropped five shots to shoot 72. Defending champion Webb Simpson had a 71 after ending play Thursday night two under par. McIlroy dropped four shots in the seven holes he completed Friday morning for a 73.

In addition to Donald, just three other players ended up under par on the first day. Mathew Goggin of Australia tied Donald at 68, while Scotland's Russell Knox submitted a 69. Long-hitting Belgian Nicolas Colsaerts birdied two of his last four holes to also sneak in with a 69, the only other player besides Mickelson from the morning wave to break par.

Ten men came in at even-par 70, including Lee Westwood, who fought back from an unfortunate double bogey at the 12th when his approach hit the wicker basket atop the flagstick and bounded off the green. Others at 70 included Jason Day, 2011 Masters winner Charl Schwartzel and Rickie Fowler, who competed for the victorious USA Team in the 2009 Walker Cup at Merion.

K.J. Choi (70) posted two 35s.

First Round

A poor tee shot at the third hole cost Tiger Woods (73) a bogey, as a group consisting only of marshals observed.

Sergio Garcia (73) suffered a quadruple bogey at No. 15.

Two prominent players who struggled in the opening round regardless of which day were protagonists Woods and Sergio Garcia of Spain, who began championship week with a gentlemanly handshake that signified that they had put aside their differences — which had led to some unfortunate words from Garcia for which he apologized.

Garcia went from putting his foot in his mouth to wanting to bite his driver in half. At the twin terrors along Golf House Road, the 14th and 15th, the par-4 holes that skirt the pavement and out of bounds on the left, Garcia sent souvenirs into the gallery. At the former, his foot slipped and he pulled his tee shot. At the 15th, it was a duck-hook. He made a double-bogey 6 and a quadruple-bogey 8, and it was quite a display of pluck that he managed to rally to a 73 thanks to a 25-foot eagle at the par-5 second hole after making the turn. Garcia, in fact, tied Mickelson for the lowest first-nine score, a 33.

Woods, meanwhile, had nothing going, except a sore left elbow or wrist (it turned out later to be the elbow, but more on that later). Already a four-time winner on the PGA Tour in 2013, Woods appeared to hurt the arm with his second swing of the championship as he tried to power his

Rickie Fowler (70) used his local knowledge.

Branden Grace (70) was one of 10 men to shoot par.

Tim Clark (70) avoided his 21st straight round over par.

Two-time champion Ernie Els (71) was over par.

approach to the first green out of Merion's meddlesome rough. Pain creased his face again after he attempted to hit a 5-wood out of the right rough at the long par-4 fifth hole. Three more times before play was halted Thursday he grimaced in pain after swings. It probably hurt just as much that he bogeyed three of his first five holes and never really got in a rhythm.

"My left arm didn't feel very good on that shot … a few shots. But, overall, it was not too bad a round," Woods said before grabbing a quick bite and then embarking on his second round. "I certainly had two three-putts, a boatload of putts, or the round could have easily been under par. So that's good heading into this afternoon."

There was a follow-up question for the pre-championship favorite about his arm. What prompted his reaction? What did he feel?

"Pain," Woods replied, drawing laughs.

Merion had many participants doubled over from gut punches.

The field averaged 74.308, higher than expected given the considerable rain. Graeme McDowell, one of the pre-championship favorites, the 2010 U.S. Open champion and 2012 joint runner-up, stumbled to a 76. Jim Furyk, who grew up in nearby Lancaster, Pa., was another stroke

First Round

Defending champion Webb Simpson (71) sent a long putt on its way at the par-3 17th.

Jason Day (70) made five birdies.

back at 77. The 2011 British Open champion, Darren Clarke posted 80, one of 10 scores at least that high.

Things even got a bit ridiculous. On the way to a 72, Carl Pettersson had begun his backswing on his second shot from the fairway at the fifth when another ball came out of nowhere and struck his, moving it. Pettersson was able to stop his swing in time and replaced the ball. It turns out that Brandon Crick of McCook, Neb., had hooked his ball from No. 2 into the fifth fairway.

"By far the strangest thing that ever happened to me on a golf course," Pettersson said.

Mickelson, meanwhile, looked as if he was feeling no pain. That's not quite how the day began. When he three-putted his first hole, the par-4 11th, from 40 feet, a long and trying day looked in store for the four-time major winner.

From there, however, he played impeccably, even as he began to fatigue.

Mickelson returned to level par when he holed a 10-foot birdie at the par-3 13th. He added three

Justin Rose (71) blasted out of a greenside bunker at the ninth hole to save par.

more birdies at the first, seventh and ninth holes. At No. 7, he went wicker hunting, and his 9-iron stopped 2 feet from the hole. A 5-iron at the 237-yard par-3 ninth set up a sweeping right-to-left breaking 30-footer that Mickelson somehow negotiated.

In between, he made two unconscious par saves at the fifth and sixth holes.

"I totally get what he was doing, going home, being there for his daughter and being a dad," said Stricker, who announced in January he was cutting back his playing schedule to spend more time at home and was only making his seventh start of the year at the U.S. Open. "Sometimes that actually takes the pressure off you because you're not here thinking about things that are going on and getting yourself worked up.

"Phil has incredible talent, and it was fun to see him do what he did," added Stricker, who opened with a 71. "Of course, it does help when you have your own plane. I heard some fans out there yelling 'US Airways.' That made us laugh."

Steve Stricker (71), in just his seventh event of the year.

Matt Kuchar (74) had little to smile about.

Italy's Matteo Manassero (75) was five over par.

Rory McIlroy (73) missed a birdie try at the 10th.

"He played very well," added Bradley, the 2011 PGA champion who struggled to a 77. "He missed the fairway and laid up. He's putting awesome, made a couple of ridiculous up-and-downs. He's had a crazy 24 hours."

Well, it wasn't that crazy. Or even novel. Nicklaus, who shares the U.S. Open record with four victories, was famous for jetting off occasionally in the middle of a tournament to be on hand for his children's sporting events or other special occasions. But like Mickelson he could afford to do it because he'd completed his homework in the days leading up to championship week rather than waiting to "cram" for the exam.

"This was as easy as this golf course is going to play," Mickelson said, conceding that his half of the draw had gotten a break with the weather and softness of the course. "We had very little wind, there was some but very little. We had soft fairways, soft greens, and we had no mud balls. So we had the best opportunity to score low. And we are all strug-

Australia's John Senden (70) blasted out of the sand here at the seventh during an up-and-down opening round.

gling because it's such a penalizing golf course. It's penalizing if you miss the fairways, very difficult if you miss the greens, and it's not a given to two-putt on these greens. They're some of the most pitched greens we have ever seen and they're very quick."

Of course, Lefty just loved it.

When he made the turn after his first eight holes, Mickelson spied USGA Executive Director Mike Davis eating lunch at the clubhouse clinging close to the first teeing ground. There was a backup on the tee, so Mickelson walked over to Davis and complimented him on Merion's championship presentation.

"I told him that this is the best setup I've ever seen for a U.S. Open," Mickelson said. "I think that what I love about Merion and what they did to Merion in the setup is they made the hard holes even harder. They moved the tees back on the more difficult holes, which made it even tougher pars. And I love that because, if you're playing well, you're going to be able to make pars and you're going to be able to separate yourself from the field by making pars.

"But on the easy holes, they didn't trick them up and take away your birdie opportunities. They gave you birdie opportunities to get those strokes back. So we have really hard holes and we have some very good birdie opportunities. I think it's the best U.S. Open setup I've ever seen, and that's what I was telling him."

And then he was showing everyone just how much he enjoyed it, forging just his fifth inter-round lead in 85 U.S. Open rounds.

Of course, that put an early target on his back, more pressure on his shoulders, and just 18 holes into the championship the left-handed star couldn't escape questions about his 22 previous U.S. Open starts that yielded those five seconds, nine top-10s and 11 top-25 finishes.

He didn't flinch.

"If I'm able — and I believe I will — if I'm able to ultimately win a U.S. Open, I would say that it's great," Mickelson said, the sun shining on his face as the clouds gave way. "Because I will have had … a win and five seconds. But if I never get that win, then it would be a bit heartbreaking."

Billy Horschel (139) hit all 18 greens in regulation on the way to a 3-under 67 and a share of the lead.

It was both surprising and logical that Billy Horschel could author a historic performance in the second round of the 113th U.S. Open Championship.

A fourth-year professional from Jacksonville Beach, Fla., Horschel fired an impeccable 3-under-par 67 under breezy and partly cloudy skies to tie Phil Mickelson for both the low round of the championship and, as it turned out when Mickelson birdied his final hole of the day, the 36-hole lead at 1-under 139.

Seldom do statistics — beyond score, of course — come to create headlines, especially in a major championship. But the nuts and bolts of Horschel's round were so astounding that it sent the United States Golf Association historians digging deep into the record books to assess their significance.

As it turned out, they had to go back to Johnny Miller's final-round 63 in the 1973 U.S. Open at Oakmont to find anyone who had hit all 18 greens in regulation in the championship. Records for golf minutia only go back to 1989. When David Graham carded a closing 67 to win the 1981 U.S. Open at Merion, he used his putter on all 18 greens, but he was not credited with hitting all of them because three were just barely off the putting surface and on the fringe cut.

"No, I was not in the zone, trust me," said Horschel, 26, a member of the victorious 2007 USA Walker Cup Team, who had to play 29 holes in all on Friday due to Thursday's weather delays. "This golf course, even though it's soft, is still a tough golf course. I know what in the zone is for me. I don't get nervous. I just see the shot and go. And I saw the shot, and I went with it, but I was still nervous with a lot of them. Your misses here can be bad if you miss in the wrong spots."

But he never did miss. A three-putt at the tiny par-3 13th led to his only bogey against four birdies, including a 15-footer at the home hole after an approach that sent the ball just skirting by the hole.

"I didn't know I hit every green until I walked off 18," Horschel said. "It's a cool thing. But like I said, it's not the first time I've hit all 18 greens. I've done it plenty of times in my career. Obviously, it's at a U.S. Open, but I think the softness of the greens helped that."

The surprise aspect of Horschel's performance was that he admittedly is not the most patient golfer, a trait that usually is necessary for navigating the traditionally trying setup of a U.S. Open. His work over the last year with a sports psychologist has helped. So has the benefit of a little maturing.

"I've acquired some patience, though maybe not as much as I wish I had," Horschel said. "But I just think that the older I get, the more mature I get on the golf course, the more understanding that if I do have a bad stretch of holes, it's not that I don't hit the panic button, I just don't press right away."

After finishing 140th and 147th, respectively, on the PGA Tour money list in his first two seasons, Horschel was in the midst of a breakout season and had been among the hottest players in golf since the spring. He reeled off three consecutive top-10 finishes before earning his first victory at the Zurich Classic of New Orleans, and he posted another top-10 in the FedEx St. Jude Classic before traveling to Merion.

Furthermore, Horschel knows how to go low.

He fired a 60 at Chaska Town Course near Minneapolis on the first day of stroke-play qualifying for the 2006 U.S. Amateur, the lowest 18-hole score in USGA history.

"That was easy compared to this," he said with a big smile.

Nothing was easy for first-round leader Phil Mickelson on Friday, especially on the greens, where several scoring chances went by the wayside. Nevertheless, he somehow scraped out a 2-over 72, thanks to the 20-foot birdie putt he sank in the twilight at the difficult 18th. That earned him a tee time in the final group with Horschel.

"I got shut out today," Mickelson said. "I played really well. Even though I shot two over, it was the birdie opportunities that I didn't capitalize on. Had I made one on two or that birdie on nine or 11, I would have changed the momentum of the round.

"I don't know how anyone is going to separate too far from the field. There might be a hot round tomorrow and they might get a hot round on Sunday, but it's unlikely to be the same player."

Second Round

Billy Horschel	72 - 67	– 139	-1
Phil Mickelson	67 - 72	– 139	-1
Luke Donald	68 - 72	– 140	E
Steve Stricker	71 - 69	– 140	E
Justin Rose	71 - 69	– 140	E
John Senden	70 - 71	– 141	+1
Nicolas Colsaerts	69 - 72	– 141	+1
Charl Schwartzel	70 - 71	– 141	+1
Hunter Mahan	72 - 69	– 141	+1

The second round was suspended because of darkness at 8:27 p.m. with 68 players still on the course, and it resumed at 7:15 a.m. Saturday.

When the dust settled, Mickelson and Horschel, at 139, held a one-stroke lead over Englishmen Luke Donald and Justin Rose and American Steve Stricker, who at 46 was seeking to become the oldest U.S. Open champion — this despite playing in only six tournaments leading

Luke Donald (140) shot 72, including a hole out for birdie from the bunker at the 13th.

The clock had yet to strike midnight for Phil Mickelson (139) after a 72.

up to the championship. Stricker shot a steely 69 that included a 15-foot par save at the last. Rose, who finished in the group behind Mickelson and Stricker in what might be classified as nighttime, also had a 69, while Donald had a 72.

"That's the job of the first two rounds, to get yourself in striking distance, and tomorrow is an important day to hang around and give yourself a chance on Sunday," Rose said. "You can't get ahead of yourself on the tee shot tomorrow.

"This kind of golf course you don't know what to expect. So I don't think you're safe until you've carded your score here. You can be four or five under going into the last few holes. You don't know how the round is going to pan out, so you have to stay focused."

The 2011 Masters champion, Charl Schwartzel, after a 71, highlighted a group of four more at 1-over 141, while a large group at 143 included three former U.S. Open champions: No. 1 Tiger Woods, No. 2 Rory McIlroy and Ernie Els. Woods and McIlroy shot 70, while Els eked out a 72. In all

Steve Stricker (140) rallied with a solid 69.

Second Round

South Africa's Charl Schwartzel (141) had the gallery's attention for his tee shot on No. 9

Nicolas Colsaerts (141) was lurking after a 72.

there were 36 players within six shots.

Woods, the three-time U.S. Open winner (in 2000, 2002 and 2008) still was having problems with his left arm, a condition he aggravated at Merion and which caused him to miss his next start at the AT&T National, a PGA Tour event in which the charitable proceeds go to his own foundation. It was after the second round that Woods admitted that he hurt his elbow sometime on the way to victory at The Players in early May. Even despite this handicap, he was lurking just four behind and was girding for more East Course hardship.

"You just have to keep grinding," he said. "You just don't ever know what the winning score is going to be. You don't know if the guys are going to come back. We have a long way to go, and these conditions aren't going to get any easier."

While Mickelson and Horschel were leading the championship, two former U.S. Open champions were leading a surprising retreat out of town.

Graeme McDowell and Jim Furyk, who contended down the stretch in the 112th U.S. Open at The Olympic Club in San Francisco, figured to be in the mix again this year. But they never figured

Graeme McDowell (153) never got untracked.

out Merion's East Course, their scores kept edging north, and they ended up perhaps the two most surprising contestants dismissed after two rounds.

The cut fell at 8-over 148 with 73 of the 156 contestants qualifying for the final 36 holes. That was one stroke higher than the cut in the 1981 edition at Merion and identical to the cut in the 1971 championship here.

Merion, indeed, was proving herself timeless and wonderfully tedious.

McDowell, the 2010 U.S. Open champion, had expressed confidence earlier in the week that he could handle the East Course crucible. "I'm feeling as good physically and mentally as I ever have in my career," he said. Then he went out and suffered

A strong start helped Justin Rose (140).

Second Round

Two-time U.S. Open champion Ernie Els (143) played this shot from out of the rough.

Webb Simpson (146) dropped back after a 75.

Matt Bettencourt (143) hammered out a 71.

seven double bogeys — as many as he had made all year thus far on the PGA Tour — in rounds of 77-76–153.

"I'm temporarily dejected," said McDowell, of Northern Ireland. "This game is not about your bad weeks, it's not about — of course it's about the major championships, and you're trying to prepare yourself as well as you can coming into weeks like this. I struggled the last couple days, but that's golf, and that's the U.S. Open."

Furyk, who began the final round at Olympic in the lead and ended up tied for fourth, crashed to 77-79–156. Furyk, who grew up in nearby Lancaster, Pa., and enjoyed the company of family and dozens of friends in his gallery, was almost in shock at how poorly he played. He was one of five players who had competed in the 1989 U.S. Amateur at Merion along with Mickelson, Stricker, Geoffrey Sisk and Cliff Kresge.

"I thought myself around the golf course poorly, I putted poorly, I drove the ball poorly, just things you can't do at a U.S. Open," said Furyk, who played junior golf in the Philadelphia area.

Olympic was a long way from Merion, and not just on the map. Defending champion Webb Simpson managed to hang on after a 75 to make the cut at 146, but Michael Thompson, who tied for second with McDowell, was dealt a tough blow, shooting a 78 Friday afternoon to miss by a stroke at 149.

Henrik Stenson (140) showed grit during a 68.

Jordan Spieth, who finished as the low amateur at Olympic but competed as a professional at Merion after successfully navigating sectional qualifying, was thoroughly befuddled to the tune of 77-76–153.

"It's harder to stay patient when you're not playing well or not scoring well," Simpson said. "I tried to hang in there. I hit some really good putts coming in that hit the lip. I've had more lip-outs the last few days than I've had at any point in my career. So, hopefully, on the weekend they'll start falling."

Patience is a virtue common to all U.S. Open champions, but sometimes that isn't enough by itself, as many former winners could attest.

Angel Cabrera, the 2007 champion at Oakmont, near Pittsburgh, didn't find the eastern end of the state of Pennsylvania nearly as welcoming to his power game. A second-round 81 left him at 155. Lucas Glover, who won in 2009, finished a stroke higher, his 82 resulting in a 156 total. Michael Campbell of New Zealand, who triumphed in 2005 at Pinehurst No. 2, site of next year's U.S. Open, suffered three doubles and a triple bogey in a second-round 78 that left him at 154. Campbell, 44, missed his eighth cut in the nine championships since his victory, and in 15 U.S. Opens, he has completed 72 holes just four times.

Other casualties among the major winners:

Geoff Ogilvy (144) bounced back from a rough start.

Martin Kaymer (148) made the cut on the number.

Second Round

Amateur Cheng-Tsung Pan (144) shot his second 72.

Matt Kuchar (147) made the cut with a late burst.

Michael Kim (142) was low amateur after a 70.

Masters champions Zach Johnson (151) and Jose Maria Olazabal (156), PGA champions David Toms, Y.E. Yang and Keegan Bradley, all of whom carded 152, and British Open champions Stewart Cink (150) and Darren Clarke (155). Another past British Open winner, Louis Oosthuizen, withdrew prior to the second round after opening with a 75, citing an unspecified injury.

Not all the major winners crumbled at the end, though. One notable exception was 2003 Masters winner Mike Weir, who has struggled in recent years with injuries. He had to par his last hole, the tough 18th, to extend to nine years his streak of making the cut, and he came through with 76–148.

Four amateurs made the cut, the most since 2004, and two of the quartet stood among the top 20

Gonzalo Fernandez-Castano (143) played steady golf.

U.S. Amateur winner Steven Fox (150) missed the cut.

heading into the second half of the championship.

Leading the way was Michael Kim, a native of Seoul, Korea, who competes for the University of California-Berkeley golf team. An impressive second-round 70 left him at 3-over 143, tied for 13th place with a group that included Woods and McIlroy. The last amateur to win the U.S. Open was Johnny Goodman in 1933.

"It's pretty cool," said Kim, 19, playing in his first U.S. Open. "I've just been really steady, hitting a decent amount of fairways and greens. I've been putting pretty well. These greens are really tricky, and I think putting is one of my strengths, and it's been working so far."

Though he stumbled to the finish line after lingering among the top 10, Cheng-Tsung Pan, 21, of Bradenton, Fla., finished at 4-over 144 after a pair of 72s. A native of Chinese Taipei who completed an All-American season at the University of Washington, Pan played his final five holes Saturday morning in four over par.

Tiger Woods (143) wasn't happy with this putt on No. 9.

Lee Westwood (147) struggled to a 77 in the second round.

Jerry Kelly (143) posted 73.

Kevin Phelan, 22, a dual citizen of Ireland and the U.S., made the cut in his second U.S. Open appearance with rounds of 71-77–148. Michael Weaver, 22, a teammate of Kim's and the U.S. Amateur runner-up, shot a pair of 74s in his U.S. Open debut and earned a weekend pass at 148.

U.S. Amateur champion Steven Fox of Hendersonville, Tenn., fell short after touring Merion in 76-74–150.

None of the 20 players who made it through local and sectional qualifying made the cut, the first time since 1997.

Heading into the third round of the championship, the co-leaders had to digest a sobering statistic: in the 112 previous U.S. Opens, the 36-hole pacesetter had won just 28 times.

"I just like being in the mix," said Mickelson, enjoying the 30th occasion of his career when he held the midway lead. "I think it's fun having a chance heading into the weekend. The way I have control off the tee and as good as the putter is, even though it didn't show today, I'm very excited about the opportunity this weekend. There are a lot of players right there, around par or a couple over."

Bubba Watson (147) hit his third shot up to the green at the 18th.

Said Horschel, who was out front after 36 holes for the third time in his career: "I've gotten a lot more comfortable with that [leading]. Like I've said in the past, I've felt more comfortable coming from behind, something I've always done throughout my career. There's not many tournaments that I've led going into the final round. It's just all about limiting distractions and not thinking about scenarios, what happens if I win or anything. It's just focusing on what I do best, and that's playing golf."

Playing golf was about to get much more interesting for everyone still standing at Merion Golf Club.

"It's not as easy as people think," Simpson said. "I heard 15, 16 under floating around. And it's going to be a normal U.S. Open winning score, I think."

"It tests every aspect of your game," said McIlroy, the 2011 champion. "There were people talking about 62s and 63s at the start of the week and, I mean, I never saw that at all. I still think that something very little under par is going to win this week. Or if not that, around even par."

Adam Scott (147) wasn't able to make a move.

Rory McIlroy (143) earned a tie for ninth with a 70.

Phil Mickelson (209) was pleased after a birdie at the 17th gave him the 54-hole lead by one stroke.

113th U.S. OPEN
Third Round

All that separated Phil Mickelson from his long awaited and fiercely coveted U.S. Open title was 18 holes of golf and an exorcism of his personal history in the championship.

Hard to say which was going to be more difficult to overcome.

Mickelson had thrust himself into the spotlight even before the first shot had been struck in the 113th U.S. Open Championship, when he made the decision to be home in California for his daughter's eighth-grade commencement rather than further study what was proving to be a classic U.S. Open examination. The gesture had made him an even greater sentimental favorite. When he improbably seized the first-round lead on little sleep, the cascade of hope from the galleries washed over him with more force than the rains that had dampened Merion Golf Club.

A closing birdie in Round 2 after a trying afternoon of near-misses had allowed him to retain a share of the lead. Now there he was alone at the top again, as if fate were intervening, as if Jones and Hogan and Nicklaus and Trevino were somehow, through the echoes of their past glories at Merion, pulling him across the finish line that in years before had disappeared like a mirage whenever he got close enough to touch it.

It wasn't the most picturesque display of golf Mickelson orchestrated in the third round of the championship, but it was sufficient. With his 70 strokes Saturday on Merion's East Course, level par, the star-crossed left-hander remained the only player under par.

"It's got the makings to be something special," Mickelson said after forging his first solo 54-hole lead in the championship. "But I still have to go out and perform, and play some of my best golf."

Indeed, there was something special brewing. But in the churning cauldron of a U.S. Open, on a golf course as obstinate as any in recent memory, and with the image of five silver medals dangling in his psyche as reminders of all the disappointments he had sustained, Mickelson surely knew — as did most anyone else — that something potentially dreary and dispiriting was lurking, too.

Only a victory ... on Father's Day ... on the day of his 43rd birthday ... could fulfill all these markers of destiny before him. Mickelson would have to sleep on the most important 54-hole lead of his life — though he admitted he doesn't sleep well during the week of a major championship — and try hard not to let the pressure of the moment overwhelm him.

"I don't think I feel any more pressure than anybody else who wants to win ... a major championship, the U.S. Open," Mickelson said, deflecting the what-if queries as best he could, knowing they had to be asked. "But it would certainly mean a lot to me that this is a tournament for years I've had opportunities, I've come close to, and it would mean a lot tomorrow if I could play some of my best golf. Certainly if I can play the way I have been playing."

Sunday's final round was set to begin with eight players within five strokes of Mickelson's 1-under 139 total, not a particularly large posse, but all of its members capable spoilers.

Hunter Mahan, 2011 Masters champion Charl Schwartzel and part-time golfer and full-time threat Steve Stricker were a stroke back. Justin

Third Round

Phil Mickelson	67 - 72 - 70 – 209	-1
Hunter Mahan	72 - 69 - 69 – 210	E
Charl Schwartzel	70 - 71 - 69 – 210	E
Steve Stricker	71 - 69 - 70 – 210	E
Justin Rose	71 - 69 - 71 – 211	+1
Luke Donald	68 - 72 - 71 – 211	+1
Billy Horschel	72 - 67 - 72 – 211	+1
Jason Day	70 - 74 - 68 – 212	+2
Rickie Fowler	70 - 76 - 67 – 213	+3
*Michael Kim	73 - 70 - 71 – 214	+4

Rose, Luke Donald and second-round co-leader Billy Horschel were next at 211, while Jason Day was three behind. Rickie Fowler, who charged to Saturday's low round, a 67 that tied the best of the week, moved up 28 places and was alone in ninth place with a 213 total.

Each one harbored his own quiet desperation for the title, especially considering that only Schwartzel had a major to his credit.

"The major, the win would be — it would be unbelievable," said Stricker, who, at 46, was seeking to wrest from Hale Irwin the title of oldest U.S. Open winner. "But I'm not trying to think about that yet. I'm just trying to execute the shots that I know how to do and take one shot at a time and go from there."

While the top nine were pondering their respective fates and hoping for the best, the guy sitting in 10th place was trying to keep his head from spinning.

Of course, what would a U.S. Open at Merion be without the emergence of a young challenger? In 1950, it was Bob Toski in his first U.S. Open, finishing tied for 20th. In 1971, amateur Jim Simons, a Wake Forest All-American, shot a third-round 65 and held the 54-hole lead. His eventual tie for fifth was the highest finish by an amateur since Jack Nicklaus tied for fourth in 1961. And in 1981, it was 1978 U.S. Amateur champion John Cook who made a spirited bid before ending up tied for fourth place.

Hunter Mahan (210) surged within one after a 69.

113th U.S. Open

Charl Schwartzel (210) blasted from a bunker at the 17th.

At the 113th U.S. Open, amateur Michael Kim, an All-American golfer for the University of California-Berkeley, took his turn in a starring role. Kim, 19, raced up the leader board with a string of birdies and found himself in the lofty heights of contending for the championship.

The run began at the short par-4 10th, and Kim quickly added two more birdies at the 12th and 13th, the latter from 5 feet to move into a tie for fifth place at one over par with Mickelson, Rose, Horschel and Ian Poulter.

He wasn't done, gathering yet another birdie from 14 feet at the tough par-4 15th, elevating the native of Korea to a tie for third place at even par with Mickelson and Rose.

"I didn't really know what to expect coming in, honestly; just wanted to make the cut," said Kim, who won four college tournaments during the 2012-13 season. "I thought that would be a pretty good week. And I did that this morning, and it feels great."

Amateur Michael Kim (214) impressed with a 71.

45

Third Round

Justin Rose (211) teed off on Merion's historic home hole and posted a 71.

Though now a part-time player, Steve Stricker (210) put himself in the mix with a 70.

Kim, who was born in Korea but since has become an American citizen after his family moved to the U.S. when he was seven, said he might have gotten a bit ahead of himself after the birdies started flying in.

"I kept looking at the leader board, not because I wanted to know how I was doing in the tournament, but it was so cool to see my name next to those names like Mickelson, Donald, Schwartzel … it was just an incredible feeling," said Kim, who got a huge assist throughout the week from local caddie LaRue Temple, who had worked 16 years at Merion. "But, yeah, I kind of went through that what-if situation in my head. What if I won or what if I did this?

"Then, of course, I hit a terrible tee shot on the next hole."

That tee shot led to a bogey 5 at the 16th, followed by a double bogey at the par-3 17th. For good measure, he succumbed to one more 5, another bogey, at the home hole to come home in 71 and 4-over 214, good for solo 10th place.

It was also good for some lifetime bragging rights and storytelling, for well behind the youngster were the No. 1 and No. 2 players in the world, hopelessly out of the championship after playing together for a third round.

Tiger Woods and Rory McIlroy each birdied the first hole Saturday to quickly climb within three of the lead, but, shockingly, that was all the electricity they could muster.

McIlroy, the 2011 U.S. Open champion, bogeyed three of his next four holes and cratered to a 75, equaling his second-worst score in his brief experience in the championship.

"You get on the wrong side of the greens, and it's just frightening because I didn't feel like I played too badly," the young Ulsterman said. "I missed a few shots here and there, and I was trying on every shot out there, and I was trying to get myself back into it, but it's tough. If you're just not a hundred percent on top of your game, it's going to expose some of your flaws or weaknesses."

Woods, five years removed from the last of

Third Round

The tough rough led to a closing double bogey and 71 for Luke Donald (211).

Rickie Fowler (213) had Saturday's low round, a 67.

his three U.S. Open titles, appeared truculently in command of his ball-striking, hitting 13 of 14 fairways and 13 greens in regulation. But he struggled to position his ball close to the hole on the deceptively sloped greens, and when he did err, he paid the penalty to the tune of a 76, matching his highest U.S. Open score as a professional. Only a 77 in the third round of the 1996 championship at Oakland Hills Country Club, near Detroit, was worse, but he was still an amateur then.

At 9-over 219, he was 10 strokes back.

"At least I started well," Woods quipped after failing to break 70 for the 11th time in a row on the weekend at a major championship. "I just couldn't get a feel for the greens. Some putts were slow, some were fast, and I had a tough time getting my speed right.

"It is certainly frustrating because I was feeling like I was playing well this week, and I just didn't make the putts I needed to make."

Frustration, with a healthy side of anxiety and humble pie for dessert, was the special of the day at Merion.

Billy Horschel (211) hung tough with a 72.

Jason Day (212) played the par 3s in two under for a 68.

And this was among the leaders.

If nothing else, the pretenders got demoted; 30 players had begun the third round within five strokes, and that was whittled to 10 as scores edged upward under bright sunshine.

A war of attrition emerged as the best strategy, and recognition of such along with enough proper execution eventually created a logjam near the top. Seven players claimed at least a share of the lead at some point in the round as Merion gave up some scoring in her soft middle. But it was how the fire-breathing finishing holes, 17 and 18, were navigated that determined the complexion of the race heading into the final round.

Just about everyone got burned. The 17th, a par 3, was playing 253 yards; the 18th, a par 4, measured 530 yards, framed by deep rough.

Gonzalo Fernandez-Castano (215) took aim at the 16th.

Henrik Stenson (215) tried to get a read on the greens.

David Lingmerth (216) shot his second straight 71.

John Senden (215) slid a bit with 74.

Charlie Hoffman (216) made a chip-in birdie at No. 4.

Mahan and Schwartzel each flirted with bettering the low round of the week but finished bogey-bogey for respective 69s. Rose went bogey-bogey for a 71, and his English compatriot, Luke Donald, staggered in bogey-double bogey that dropped him to 71 and out of the lead he had battled for so assiduously for the first 16 holes.

"If you hit one bad shot on any of those [final] four holes, it generally leads to a bogey," Rose said. "They're very unforgiving from that point of view. So you've just got to play a clean nine or 10 shots … in regulation. If you don't do that, you are really struggling for par. So it asks the questions, for sure."

There were some survivors. Overcoming a double bogey at the par-3 ninth when he hit his tee shot into Cobb's Creek, Stricker steadied himself to play two under the rest of the way for a 70. Day played the last two holes in even par with a birdie and bogey in a handsome 68 that gave him his second realistic chance at the U.S. Open title

Ian Poulter (215) looked a bit dejected after his bunker shot at the ninth hole.

in three years. And Horschel, the youngster in the group, managed to scratch out 72 after a jittery early stretch. He got through the finish relatively unscathed, with just a bogey at the 18th.

"Seventeen and 18, you've got to buckle up and hit good shots," said Horschel, who would give the USGA a ball, a glove and a hat to display in its museum from his ball-striking performance the day before. "So I think tomorrow, with the pressure being on, those holes will stick out even more."

From five players under par at one juncture, now only Mickelson remained. But he wasn't immune to the bogey influenza, either.

He had relinquished the lead when he bogeyed the third and fifth holes, but consecutive birdies at the 10th and 11th, from 4 and 15 feet, respectively, got him back on track. Though he missed a chance for another birdie at the short 13th, Mickelson remained in touch with solid pars, and when he arrived at the 17th, he trailed Donald by just one shot.

Paul Casey (216) rolled to a respectable 71.

Third Round

Paul Lawrie (216) shot his first sub-par round, a 69.

Lee Westwood (216) looked cool after a bounceback 69.

Tiger Woods (219) and Rory McIlroy (218) struggled.

The next swing, with a 4-iron, took care of that.

"I just stood and admired it," Mickelson said. "It was one of the best shots I've ever hit. I mean, it just was right down the center of the green, and I was hoping it would kind of get the right bounces. It left me a beautiful uphill putt that I could be aggressive with and I made it. That was fun to do that because that's just not a hole you expect to get one back."

The birdie from 10 feet, combined with Donald's double bogey at the 18th, put Mickelson back in front. He stayed there despite his own bogey at the last after his approach rolled through the green and he chipped to 10 feet. His par attempt stopped an inch shy of the hole.

It was the first time only one player remained under par through 54 holes at the U.S. Open since 2007 at Oakmont, when not a single player was in red figures.

Mickelson couldn't have cared less about his score, just his position. For the seventh time since 1995 he was entering the final round of the U.S.

Mickelson, Donald and Horschel descended the long staircase at the 17th with caddies and officials in tow.

Open among the top five players on the leader board.

It's where he wanted to be — out front and in control of his fate if he could navigate Merion one more time with the kind of aplomb he had displayed the first three days. He talked confidently about doing just that.

"I love being in the thick of it," said Mickelson, who was the 54-hole co-leader with Kenneth Ferrie in 2006 at Winged Foot. "I've had opportunities in years past, and it has been so fun, even though it's been heartbreaking to come so close a number of times and let it slide. But I feel better equipped than I have ever felt heading into the final round of a U.S. Open. My ball-striking is better than ever, and my putting is better than it's been in years. I'm feeling great, and I love this golf course. At 43, I feel as good as I ever have.

"It's a hard challenge, but it's a lot of fun," Mickelson added with a smile. "Let's go. I can't wait to get back and playing."

And to see what fate, and the ghosts of Merion, had in store for him.

Bo Van Pelt (216) birdied Nos. 16 and 17 to salvage 72.

Justin Rose (281) had the look of a winner as he finished off a final-round 71 and won by two shots.

113th U.S. OPEN
Fourth Round

Along the turgid and tantalizing fairway corridors of matriarchal Merion Golf Club, a storybook ending came to fruition in the 113th U.S. Open Championship, just as so many people had hoped and expected. Joining the legion of U.S. Open winners from Olin Dutra and Ben Hogan to Lee Trevino and David Graham was Justin Peter Rose, born in South Africa to parents from the United Kingdom, raised in England, settled in Orlando, Fla., and nurtured by a loving father from 11 months old to be a golfer.

The son of Ken Rose showed the world just how good a golfer he was, crafting a final-round 70, even par, for a 281 total to deliver a two-stroke victory over Australia's Jason Day and sentimental favorite Phil Mickelson. While it was not the ending anyone with even the slightest streak of sympathy would have wanted — not with Mickelson and all his hard-headed resolve and hard-luck U.S. Open history permeating the air and saturating the championship narrative — it was still a fitting conclusion.

That was obvious as soon as Rose tapped in for par at the final hole and blew a kiss and pointed to the heavens in tribute to his father, who died of cancer in 2002 at age 57.

"It wasn't lost on me that today is Father's Day," said Rose, who fought to hold back tears during the trophy presentation after becoming the first U.S. Open winner from England since Tony Jacklin in 1970. "My dad was the inspiration the whole day. ... I just couldn't help but look up to the heavens and think that my old dad, Ken, had something to do with it.

"You don't often have the opportunity to dedicate victories to someone you love," Rose added. "Today was about him and being Father's Day. That was my time. The clouds had parted, it was kind of ironic. It was just a beautiful evening. And the way it worked out, I felt like I needed to do that."

Mickelson, serenaded with "Happy Birthday" on the first tee, needed to win the U.S. Open to erase all of the disappointments of his past 22 appearances in the championship. Sunday marked the fourth time he had held at least a share of the lead on the final nine holes of the championship, but the end result was that he couldn't finish it off. With a 74 and 283 total, Mickelson was relegated to his sixth runner-up finish, extending his own record that is both amazing and agonizing.

He called this latest setback the most disappointing of all, even more than his 2006 implosion at Winged Foot when he bounced his tee shot at the 72nd hole off a corporate hospitality tent and hacked his way to a double bogey that handed the trophy to Geoff Ogilvy.

Jack Nicklaus finished second in Britain's Open Championship seven times, but he also won the Claret Jug three times. Winning makes all the difference in how one assesses the final accounting.

"This is tough to swallow after coming so close," Mickelson sighed. "This was my best chance of all. I had a golf course I really liked. I felt this was as good an opportunity as you could ask for. It really hurts. At 43, and coming so close five times, it would have changed the way I look at this tournament altogether and the way I would have looked at my record in the U.S. Open. Except that I just keep feeling heartbreak."

Fourth Round

Jason Day (283) showed off fine form as he began his final round Sunday and notched his second runner-up finish.

Phil Mickelson (283) had the support of fans to the end.

The left-hander began the day with a one-stroke lead, but he was quickly scrambling just to remain in the fray after inexplicably untidy double bogeys at the third and fifth holes. "Those were costly doubles," Mickelson said. "I should have made bogeys on those holes and I let them become doubles."

That opened the door to what became a four-man tussle among Mickelson, Rose, Day, who tied for second after a 71, and Hunter Mahan, who each grabbed at least a piece of first place during the mostly cloudy but warm afternoon. Meanwhile, Luke Donald and Charl Schwartzel drowned in a sea of early bogeys, and Steve Stricker all but eliminated himself at the second hole when he lost two balls out of bounds and made a triple-bogey 8.

Mahan, playing in the final pairing with Mickelson, stayed in the hunt with a steady display of golf, making par on 13 of the first 14 holes before running out of gas and shooting 75 to drop into a tie for fourth. Day, coming off a disappointing

Fourth Round

Justin Rose	71 - 69 - 71 - 70 – 281	+1
Jason Day	70 - 74 - 68 - 71 – 283	+3
Phil Mickelson	67 - 72 - 70 - 74 – 283	+3
Jason Dufner	74 - 71 - 73 - 67 – 285	+5
Ernie Els	71 - 72 - 73 - 69 – 285	+5
Billy Horschel	72 - 67 - 72 - 74 – 285	+5
Hunter Mahan	72 - 69 - 69 - 75 – 285	+5
Luke Donald	68 - 72 - 71 - 75 – 286	+6
Steve Stricker	71 - 69 - 70 - 76 – 286	+6
Hideki Matsuyama	71 - 75 - 74 - 67 – 287	+7
Nicolas Colsaerts	69 - 72 - 74 - 72 – 287	+7
G. Fernandez-Castano	71 - 72 - 72 - 72 – 287	+7
Rickie Fowler	70 - 76 - 67 - 74 – 287	+7

third-place finish at the Masters after leading with three holes to play, fought back to level par for the championship after a birdie at the short par-4 10th hole and was in it until the end. He bogeyed the 18th in a bid to catch Rose, attempting to hole out his third shot from the greenside bunker.

"I was proud of how I played," said Day, 25, who relishes the challenge of the U.S. Open. "Yeah, I like these tournaments where you have to fight your way through all the troubles and just be tough. The U.S. Open isn't just about hitting the shots. It's about using your brain. It's about guts.

"As long as I keep knocking on the door, I think I'll win a major here soon."

Tell that to Mickelson, who didn't win despite delivering one of his signature strokes of brilliance that seemed to auger a favorable outcome. After pulling his tee shot into the right rough at the par-4 10th, Lefty unsheathed one of the five wedges in his bag and holed the next shot from 75 yards for an eagle to return to even par for the championship. He leapt in the air and then raised his arms, his lead restored and a virtual knockout blow delivered to his foes. Or so it seemed.

"To see that ball go in, I really thought that I was in a good position," Mickelson said.

Rose had other ideas. He had just three-putted the 11th when Mickelson pulled his Mickelson,

Mickelson celebrated an unlikely eagle at the 10th hole.

Fourth Round

Hunter Mahan (285) faced this delicate pitch shot at the par-5 fourth hole Sunday. He closed with a 75.

Jason Dufner (285) bolted up the board with a 67.

and his response was to make birdie at the next two holes, a 4-footer at the 12th and a 20-footer at the 13th to retake the lead.

"I just went about it in a 'one foot in front of the other' fashion," Rose said.

Unfortunately for Mickelson, he followed with a few fatal missteps, none more painful than the bogey he suffered at the par-3 13th when he overshot the green with a hooking wedge shot into deep hay and couldn't get a 20-foot par putt to drop after a decent hack out. Another bogey at the 15th, again after a poor wedge shot, kept him in pursuit mode, and he failed to birdie any of the three closing holes to forge a tie with Rose.

Though he, too, struggled on the way in, suffering bogeys at the 14th and 16th, Rose covered the two closing holes in the requisite par total — after playing them in three over the first three days.

At the par-3 17th he ripped his tee shot with a 5-iron hole high and neatly two-putted.

All that was left was the iconic 18th hole, and

Two-time winner Ernie Els (285) got close after a 69.

Rose split the fairway with his tee shot. When he arrived at his golf ball, the famous Ben Hogan plaque was a few paces nearby commemorating his pure 1-iron shot at the 72nd hole of the 1950 U.S. Open that led to a tie and his eventual win in a playoff.

And almost as if orchestrated by a stagehand in a play, the sun broke through the clouds, illuminating the glory of Merion and the potential glory in Rose's hands. He striped a 4-iron that bounded right next to the hole but then raced through the green. He used a fairway metal for his recovery shot and nearly holed it, the ball stopping inches away. He tapped in to finish at 1-over 281.

His work completed, all Rose could do was wait to see if he'd be the fifth man in as many U.S. Opens at Merion to win in come-from-behind fashion. When Mickelson's birdie pitch shot from in front of the green bounded past the hole, Rose had won his first major and had broken England's major drought dating to Nick Faldo's victory in the 1996 Masters.

Billy Horschel (285) stood out with his clothes.

Fourth Round

Luke Donald (286) had to disrobe a bit to escape the hazard at the fourth hole.

Nicolas Colsaerts (287) was among the leaders in driving.

Gonzalo Fernandez-Castano (287) tied for 10th.

"When I walked over the hill and saw my drive sitting perfectly in the middle of the fairway, with the sun coming out, it was kind of almost fitting," Rose said. "And I just felt like at that point it was a good iron shot onto the green, two putts — like Hogan did — and possibly win this championship. So I felt like I did myself justice, and probably put enough of a good swing where Ben Hogan might have thought it was a decent shot, too."

It was better than decent. It might one day be considered career defining.

"I really targeted Merion. I've been striving my whole life, really, to win a major championship," said Rose, who needed 37 major starts to break through. "I felt like this tournament really began to be on my radar as the one major championship that would suit me the most. I had always felt good at Augusta, always dreamed about winning the [British] Open Championship. But I thought this one actually might have been my best chance.

"I just love it when a plan comes together. It's how this week felt, to be honest."

Well, one man's successful plan leaves all others scuttled.

Exactly five years to the day of his last U.S. Open title at Torrey Pines, Tiger Woods finished off a desultory performance with a closing 74 and 13-over 293 total, joining a group in a tie for 32nd

The orange-clad Rickie Fowler (287) had to hit from the hazard at the par-4 fifth hole, leading to a bogey.

that included defending champion Webb Simpson and 2006 U.S. Open winner Geoff Ogilvy. The No. 1 player in the world, Woods submitted his worst finishing score in relation to par in the U.S. Open since he turned professional after the 1996 U.S. Amateur and matching his worst score in any major.

"There's always a lesson to be learned in every tournament whether you win or lose," Woods, 37, said. "I'll look back at the things I did right and the things I did wrong."

Two players added 67s to the list of those claiming lowest round of the week. American Jason Dufner played his first 13 holes in five under par, the lowest anyone had gotten under par all week. But he lost a ball out of bounds at the 14th to suffer a triple bogey. Hideki Matsuyama of Japan, who had just turned professional in April, also lost a bit of steam at the 14th, making bogey after reaching four under. Dufner tied for fourth at 5-over 285

Steve Stricker (286) struggled early, closing with 76.

Fourth Round

Brandt Snedeker (290) finished well back.

with Mahan, Billy Horschel, who shot 74, and two-time U.S. Open winner Ernie Els, who made a stirring bid with a closing 69. Matsuyama claimed a share of 10th place at 287.

The last time a U.S. Open golf course held the field to no better than a 67 was in the 2007 championship at Oakmont Country Club, near Pittsburgh. Was it any wonder, then, that proclamations about Merion's timeless relevance were so pervasive?

Thirty-two years ago David Graham had won

Charl Schwartzel (288) had a tough final day and nearly fell into a bunker at the ninth hole.

John Huh (290) enjoyed a good debut in the U.S. Open, tied for 17th, after a final-round 71.

at seven under par. Ten years before that, in 1971, even par had earned Jack Nicklaus and Lee Trevino a tie at the top that Trevino broke the next day in an epic playoff. Yet here was tiny Merion, less than 7,000 yards, pitching a shutout on red numbers, an unthinkable development when the opponents are now bigger and stronger, golf balls fly straighter and farther, and clubs are more forgiving and calibrated to each player's micro-tweaked swing.

And this was a Merion East Course that had been doused with nearly 7 inches of rain. As England's Lee Westwood, who tied for 15th, claimed on Twitter: "If Merion would have played dry this week like the USGA wanted, it would have been impossible."

The final statistical numbers on Merion were breathtaking — as in, Merion had every player holding his breath from every tee shot to every hole out, no matter the distance. The field averaged 74.546 for the week and made more than twice as

Lee Westwood (289) ended up tied for 15th.

Fourth Round

Rose made a birdie at the 13th.

many bogeys (2,079) as it did birdies and eagles (988). The 18th hole didn't yield a birdie in the final two rounds.

Only 11 eagles were recorded, and that included Mickelson's unlikely hole-out at the 10th and the first ace in a U.S. Open at Merion by 31-year-old Texan Shawn Stefani at the par-3 17th hole. Stefani rebounded from an 85 in the third round to record a closing 69 assisted by a magic 4-iron shot from 213 yards that he improbably banked off the left hillside, across the green and into the hole.

"I didn't know what to do but jump up and down for joy," Stefani said after making his first hole-in-one in tournament play and the 43rd known ace in U.S. Open history. Stefani kissed the hill that delivered his ace before proceeding to the 18th tee, drawing a raucous ovation.

Merion rightfully took its bows, too. And so did the USGA, whose own audacious plan to

Rose and his caddie, Mark Fulcher, walked alone together at the 17th.

David Lingmerth (290) gave it a ride.

David Hearn (291) studied this putt carefully.

John Senden (289) tied for 15th with Lee Westwood.

Martin Laird (291) finished strong with a 68.

bring the U.S. Open back to august Merion was an unqualified success.

"The last time we had a U.S. Open here was 1981 [and] we were still using persimmon [drivers] and balata [balls]. And so much has happened since that period of time. Just how you play the game," said Mike Davis, executive director of the USGA and lead man in the setup of Merion, to begin a summation of the week. "I think there was

Fourth Round

Low amateur Michael Kim (290) with LaRue Temple.

that natural tendency to say, 'Well, Merion's been passed by.' And I really do think that … a lot of people said there's just too many short holes to test these players.

"But at the end of it, you have to still remember that it's a 4¼-inch hole that you have to get it into. And it's not all about distance. I'm telling you, we could play an 8,500-yard course with straightaways, and these guys would have no trouble. It's when you all of a sudden get holes that move different directions, unlevel lies, wind, some blindness, greens that undulate — that's what tests these players. They can hit it a long way and they can hit it straight, but it's this type of architecture that you really have to think your way around it.

"Like a lot of us thought, it stood the test of time," Davis added. "Merion for those that really studied Merion, it's always been short relative to other championship sites, and it's always, always held its own. It's always a great test of golf. And we knew it would be."

And, of course, Merion produced a proper champion. There was no bloom off Merion's rose, but it did foster the bloom of one very special Rose.

Mickelson ran up to see if his pitch shot to tie Rose went in. His reaction told the result.

Rose pointed to the heavens in tribute to his father after holing out at the 18th.

The happy champion of the 113th U.S. Open, with the trophy and the iconic Merion basket atop the flagstick.

113th U.S. OPEN
The Champion

One of the last golf lessons father ever delivered to son was prior to the 131st Open Championship at Muirfield, Scotland, in the summer of 2002. Justin Rose found himself in a first-round pairing with Tiger Woods, and the English youngster was a bit on edge, to say the least, playing alongside the No. 1 player in the world and the winner of the year's first two majors.

Ken Rose, 57, who had given his son a plastic club before the child's first birthday and had served as coach and mentor, always had known just what to say. He had that way not only with his boy, but with just about anyone he met. Five years earlier, as his 17-year-old son was bursting onto the big stage at the 1998 Open Championship at Royal Birkdale, the elder Rose was proving himself to be charming and genuine as the media crowded around him, explaining, wryly, that the family lived in a place called Hook, "next to the town of Slice."

But by 2002, Ken, who was an outstanding squash and tennis player and had been such a huge inspiration to his boy, was dying of leukemia. Still, he knew just what to tell Justin before that big round.

"My dad had a great understanding of me," Rose recalled in a recent *Golf Digest* interview. "He would just look into my eyes and either leave me alone because I was ready, or decide if I needed something from him. I remember he gave me a great talk before I played with Tiger at Muirfield. There was a lot of hype. It came at a time when my dad was obviously not healthy, and he just said, 'We've faced far tougher things in our life than this round of golf.' It was sad, but it was also inspiring, and it gave me so much perspective. I played really well and shot 68. I always remember that lesson."

Justin Rose remembered his father with special relish and intent in the closing moments of the 113th U.S. Open Championship at Merion Golf Club. After holing out for a gutsy 70 and what would prove to be the winning score, a 1-over 281 on Merion's East Course, Rose pointed to the sky, where the clouds had just parted.

"That look was for my Dad," he said in the joyous aftermath of his first major champion triumph. "Today was about him. He was an inspiration the whole day. A lot of us came from great men and it was important for me to carry myself and do myself proud on this day. I just felt I had to do that.

"Although he'd been a big part of my life, winning the U.S. Open … that was the first real deep connection I had had with him in a very long time, and, obviously, that moment meant a lot."

Fifteen years had passed since the other truly big moment in Justin Rose's golf life filled with notable markers.

He'd broken 70 for the first time at age 11, and by 14 he carried a plus-3 handicap and had set the course record of 65 at the North Hants Club. In 1997, just 10 days past his 17th birthday, he became the youngest representative of Great Britain and Ireland in the biennial Walker Cup matches at Royal County Down Golf Club in Northern Ireland.

Then came that chilly summer day at Royal Birkdale, when Rose, nine days shy of 18, pitched in for birdie from the scrub at the final hole for a 69 and claimed a share of fourth place with Jim Furyk, Jesper Parnevik and Raymond Russell. The lad from Hampshire also found meteoric national

The Champion

renown. "Hello, England's Rose," screamed the tabloid headlines, though Rose would admit later that he, "sort of announced [himself] before I was ready to handle it."

Some questioned the wisdom of Justin turning professional immediately thereafter — though that had been his and Ken's plan all along. But the naysayers were there when Rose missed the cut in his first 21 professional events. He could have crumpled, skulked home, and let himself be forgotten, just one more prodigy who didn't pan out. But Ken Rose's kid wasn't built that way.

Instead, he worked harder, persevered, ignored the critics, and finally won his first tournament at the 2002 Nashua Masters in South Africa followed by three more wins that year: the Alfred Dunhill Championship and the British Masters on the PGA European Tour and the Chunichi Crowns in Japan.

"I honestly don't think it was until I started winning in America in 2010 that it was truly out of my system," Rose said of his early struggles that he would later label "somewhat traumatic," which makes perfect sense when so much is expected of you. "But that has been the game over the past 15 years. It has been about putting building blocks painstakingly in place. Now I'm at the point where it's a case of letting the next eight years unfold. Sure, there will be days when you can't see the game clearly, but that's why you put the blocks in place, so you don't panic."

Rose joined the PGA Tour in 2004, but he didn't break through for his first win until the 2010 Memorial Tournament, Jack Nicklaus' event at Muirfield Village Golf Club in Dublin, Ohio. A few weeks later he won Tiger's AT&T National, followed in 2011 by a FedExCup playoff event, the BMW Championship. Last year, he added a World Golf Championship title, the Cadillac Championship.

Winning the U.S. Open was just part of his natural progression over the last 15 years — and particularly over the past four since he began working with cerebral swing coach Sean Foley, whose stable includes Woods and Hunter Mahan.

Incidentally, Foley sent Rose a text on Sunday morning that brought even more poignancy to the developing events that day. It read, in part: "This is a super important day because we are the sons of great men and the fathers of beautiful children, so go out there and represent all the qualities your dad instilled in you and play and act like the man you want your son and daughter to emulate."

"You can talk about 15 years, but I feel like I've had several careers during that time, to be honest," said Rose, who also was taught by David Leadbetter after his father died. "There were the struggles and then the breaking through, winning in America, and then just a clean trajectory toward a major championship from there."

No Englishman had won the U.S. Open since Tony Jacklin in 1970, not even Nick Faldo, who won six majors, his last in 1996 when he chased down the mercurial Greg Norman in the final round of the Masters. In addition to Rose, England has produced some fine players: Lee Westwood and Luke Donald, who each ascended for a time to the top of the Official World Golf Ranking, Ian Poulter and Paul Casey. A major breakthrough was thought to be considerably overdue.

Rose, born in South Africa, but a resident of England from the age of five, acknowledged as much on the eve of the championship, telling the *Daily Mail*: "If we're really honest, I think it has now reached the point where it's down to the fact if we [the English] can handle the pressure we will win a major, and if we can't, we won't," Rose was quoted as saying. "Given all we've achieved, there's nothing to be gained from denying that fact. Speaking for myself, I look at my record over the last three years, my wins in America and what happened at the Ryder Cup, and I think I've shown I can deal with the pressure. So I've got to remain patient."

Last fall's 39th Ryder Cup, at Medinah Country Club near Chicago, may have given Rose that last bit of validation that he was ready for bigger things. Europe trailed by 6 points entering Sunday's singles matches, but they mounted a historic charge to retain the cup. Rose was instrumental in the comeback, defeating Phil Mickelson, 1 up. He sank a 12-foot par putt at the 16th to halve the hole, won the 17th with a 35-foot birdie putt, and then sank a 12-footer for birdie at the 18th for the victory, a key to Europe's remarkable rally.

"He's got loads of talent, a great game, a great work ethic," Mahan said. "He's just one of those guys that had to keep plugging along, and keep trusting himself more than anything else … just trust his abilities, because his abilities are really second to none."

"I think Justin for the last few years has been known as one of the best ball-strikers in the game. He showed that today," said Donald, who played with Rose the final day in the third-to-last pairing. "To win a U.S. Open, you have to have ultimate control of your golf ball. He did that.

"It's going to mean a lot. It's been too long, really," Donald added when asked what Rose's win meant for England. "I think we've had a lot of talent come out of England and hopefully we've broken our bad period. This will be a great week for Justin and for England."

Rose is popular among players from both sides of the Atlantic. He is polite and unassuming, much like his dad was, and is considered a good playing companion because of his easy temperament and his professionalism.

Rose's victory comes at a time of great parity in the game. He was the 18th winner in the last 19 major championships, with Rory McIlroy the only player to repeat, winning the 2011 U.S. Open and the 2012 PGA Championship.

"He had that audacious chip-in at Birkdale when he was 17 and then witnessed the difficult time he had after turning professional and all the struggles that he had, and to fight through that takes a lot of courage and what was shown was exactly that," Jacklin told BBC Radio on the Monday after. "He's a good guy and he's good for the game, and he hopefully will open the door for more British players to give us some of the same."

Actually, Rose, 32, was thinking he would like to do more of the same. If he performs like he did at Merion, you can practically count on it. Long known for having no real weakness, his all-around game was fully on display. He ranked second in fairways hit, seventh in greens in regulation, 15th in driving distance, 16th in putting.

"I think that, yeah, winning makes you hungry to do it again, because it just feels so darn good," he said.

"Winning just reminds you about why you practice hard and why you play the game. And it's not necessarily the trophy that feels so great, it's knowing that you've answered the doubts in your own head, you've answered the questions, you've taken on the challenge and you've risen to it."

USGA President Glen D. Nager with the champion, Justin Rose.

But perhaps most satisfying of all was fulfilling the immense promise on behalf of his biggest supporter, a man gone more than a decade and yet still so close to his heart and soul.

"I think my Dad always believed that I was capable of this," said Rose, a father of two children himself now. "He always also did say, when he was close to passing away, he kind of told my Mom, 'Don't worry, Justin will be OK. He'll know what to do.'"

Ken Rose was right. His boy knew just what to do, and then he went out and did it.

"What a piece of silverware to be sitting to my right," he said, looking at the gleaming U.S. Open Trophy. "It's just an incredible experience and a childhood dream come true."

118th U.S. OPEN
Merion Golf Club

June 13-16, 2013, Merion Golf Club, East Course, Ardmore, Pa.

Rd. 1	Rd. 2	Rd. 3	Rd. 4	Contestant	Rounds				Total	Prize
T16	T3	T5	1	Justin Rose	71	69	71	70	281	$1,440,000.00
T6	T20	8	T2	Jason Day	70	74	68	71	283	696,104.00
1	T1	1	T2	Phil Mickelson	67	72	70	74	283	696,104.00
T68	T31	T25	T4	Jason Dufner	74	71	73	67	285	291,406.00
T16	T13	T16	T4	Ernie Els	71	72	73	69	285	291,406.00
T33	T1	T5	T4	Billy Horschel	72	67	72	74	285	291,406.00
T33	T6	T2	T4	Hunter Mahan	72	69	69	75	285	291,406.00
T2	T3	T5	T8	Luke Donald	68	72	71	75	286	210,006.00
T16	T3	T2	T8	Steve Stricker	71	69	70	76	286	210,006.00
T16	T37	T39	T10	Hideki Matsuyama	71	75	74	67	287	168,530.00
T4	T6	T11	T10	Nicolas Colsaerts	69	72	74	72	287	168,530.00
T16	T13	T11	T10	Gonzalo Fernandez-Castano	71	72	72	72	287	168,530.00
T6	T37	9	T10	Rickie Fowler	70	76	67	74	287	168,530.00
T6	T6	T10	14	Charl Schwartzel	70	71	69	78	288	144,444.00
T6	T44	T16	T15	Lee Westwood	70	77	69	73	289	132,453.00
T6	T6	T11	T15	John Senden	70	71	74	74	289	132,453.00
T16	T20	T31	T17	John Huh	71	73	75	71	290	115,591.00
T68	T56	T25	T17	Brandt Snedeker	74	74	70	72	290	115,591.00
T68	T31	T16	T17	David Lingmerth	74	71	71	74	290	115,591.00
T46	T13	10	T17	*Michael Kim	73	70	71	76	290	Medal
T68	T44	T55	T21	Martin Laird	74	73	76	68	291	86,579.00
T132	T44	T39	T21	David Hearn	78	69	73	71	291	86,579.00
T46	T20	T31	T21	Padraig Harrington	73	71	75	72	291	86,579.00
T2	T10	T25	T21	Mathew Goggin	68	74	76	73	291	86,579.00
T46	T20	T16	T21	Bo Van Pelt	73	71	72	75	291	86,579.00
T16	T10	T11	T21	Ian Poulter	71	71	73	76	291	86,579.00
T68	T10	T11	T21	Henrik Stenson	74	68	73	76	291	86,579.00
T33	T56	T55	T28	Mike Weir	72	76	75	69	292	60,183.00
T106	T44	T31	T28	John Parry	76	71	72	73	292	60,183.00
T68	T44	T31	T28	Matt Kuchar	74	73	72	73	292	60,183.00
T68	T56	T25	T28	Morten Orum Madsen	74	74	70	74	292	60,183.00
T33	T56	T52	T32	Kevin Chappell	72	76	74	71	293	47,246.00
T68	T20	T44	T32	Geoff Ogilvy	74	70	77	72	293	47,246.00
T16	T37	T44	T32	Webb Simpson	71	75	75	72	293	47,246.00
T6	T37	T44	T32	K.J. Choi	70	76	75	72	293	47,246.00
T46	T13	T31	T32	Tiger Woods	73	70	76	74	293	47,246.00
T46	T37	T31	T32	Jamie Donaldson	73	73	73	74	293	47,246.00
T46	T20	T23	T32	Edward Loar	73	71	73	76	293	47,246.00
T16	T44	T23	T32	Bubba Watson	71	76	70	76	293	47,246.00
T106	T44	T16	T32	Paul Lawrie	76	71	69	77	293	47,246.00
T33	T44	T44	T41	Carl Pettersson	72	75	74	73	294	37,324.00
T88	T31	T39	T41	Scott Langley	75	70	75	74	294	37,324.00
T46	T13	T25	T41	Rory McIlroy	73	70	75	76	294	37,324.00
T6	T13	T25	T41	Jerry Kelly	70	73	75	76	294	37,324.00
T46	T56	T55	T45	Steven Alker	73	75	75	72	295	28,961.00
T4	T20	T44	T45	Russell Knox	69	75	77	74	295	28,961.00

113th U.S. Open

Rd. 1	Rd. 2	Rd. 3	Rd. 4	Contestant	Rounds				Total	Prize
T46	T37	T44	T45	Sergio Garcia	73	73	75	74	295	28,961.00
T33	T44	T39	T45	Bio Kim	72	75	73	75	295	28,961.00
T33	T44	T39	T45	Adam Scott	72	75	73	75	295	28,961.00
T33	T20	T31	T45	*Cheng-Tsung Pan	72	72	75	76	295	
T16	T20	T16	T45	Charley Hoffman	71	73	72	79	295	28,961.00
T46	T31	T16	T45	Paul Casey	73	72	71	79	295	28,961.00
T16	T44	T55	T53	Scott Stallings	71	76	76	73	296	23,446.00
T33	T13	T31	T53	Matt Bettencourt	72	71	76	77	296	23,446.00
T16	T56	T55	55	Dustin Johnson	71	77	75	74	297	22,561.00
T33	T56	T52	T56	Nicholas Thompson	72	76	74	76	298	21,485.00
T68	T56	T52	T56	Josh Teater	74	74	74	76	298	21,485.00
T16	T20	T23	T56	George Coetzee	71	73	77	77	298	21,485.00
T33	T31	T69	T59	Shawn Stefani	72	73	85	69	299	20,111.00
T106	T56	T60	T59	Martin Kaymer	76	72	77	74	299	20,111.00
T46	T44	T44	T59	Marcel Siem	73	71	77	78	299	20,111.00
T16	T56	T65	T62	*Kevin Phelan	71	77	78	74	300	
T88	T56	T60	T62	Matt Weibring	75	73	76	76	300	19,406.00
T68	T56	T63	64	*Michael Weaver	74	74	78	75	301	
T6	T56	68	T65	Peter Hedblom	70	78	79	75	302	18,926.00
T121	T56	T63	T65	David Howell	77	71	77	77	302	18,926.00
T46	T44	72	T67	Kevin Sutherland	73	74	84	72	303	17,965.00
T46	T56	T65	T67	John Peterson	73	75	78	77	303	17,965.00
T106	T56	T60	T67	Jim Herman	76	72	76	79	303	17,965.00
T46	T56	T60	T67	Alistair Presnell	73	75	76	79	303	17,965.00
T68	T37	T52	71	Robert Karlsson	74	72	86	73	305	17,165.00
T68	T56	T69	72	Simon Khan	74	74	82	76	306	16,844.00
T16	T31	T69	73	Kyle Stanley	71	74	85	78	308	16,523.00

Contestant				Contestant				Contestant			
Justin Hicks	76	73	149	Boo Weekley	75	76	151	Michael Campbell	76	78	154
*Chris Williams	75	74	149	Andrew Svoboda	81	70	151	Ryan Palmer	75	79	154
Michael Thompson	71	78	149	Ryan Nelson	73	78	151	Darren Clarke	80	75	155
Cliff Kresge	75	74	149	Brendan Steele	76	76	152	Angel Cabrera	74	81	155
Tim Clark	70	79	149	David Toms	75	77	152	Rikard Karlberg	78	77	155
Peter Hanson	74	75	149	Marcus Fraser	79	73	152	Wil Collins	76	79	155
Aaron Baddeley	75	74	149	Francesco Molinari	78	74	152	Harold Varner III	76	79	155
Rory Sabbatini	77	72	149	Luke Guthrie	73	79	152	Jose Maria Olazabal	75	81	156
Matteo Manassero	75	74	149	Brandon Brown	75	77	152	Jim Furyk	77	79	156
Freddie Jacobson	73	76	149	Keegan Bradley	77	75	152	Joe Ogilvie	75	81	156
Doug LaBelle II	75	74	149	Y.E. Yang	77	75	152	Lucas Glover	74	82	156
Brian Stuard	75	75	150	Marc Leishman	78	75	153	Ryan Moore	79	77	156
Morgan Hoffmann	76	74	150	Graeme McDowell	76	77	153	Russell Henley	77	80	157
Casey Wittenberg	79	71	150	Thongchai Jaidee	79	74	153	Adam Hadwin	81	76	157
Kevin Streelman	72	78	150	Branden Grace	70	83	153	Thorbjorn Olesen	79	79	158
*Steven Fox	76	74	150	Jordan Spieth	77	76	153	Yoshinobu Tsukada	78	80	158
Stewart Cink	72	78	150	Jung-Gon Hwang	75	78	153	Zack Fischer	82	76	158
Hiroyuki Fujita	76	74	150	Ryan Yip	76	77	153	Matt Harmon	78	81	159
Ted Potter Jr.	76	74	150	Mackenzie Hughes	75	78	153	Brandon Crick	81	78	159
Jaco Van Zyl	73	77	150	Geoffrey Sisk	78	75	153	Roger Tambellini	80	80	160
Chris Doak	73	77	150	Randall Hutchison	74	79	153	*Cory McElyea	81	79	160
Zach Johnson	74	77	151	John Hahn	75	78	153	Yui Ueda	78	83	161
D.A. Points	77	74	151	Estanislao Goya	71	83	154	John Nieporte	78	84	162
Sang-Moon Bae	77	74	151	Scott Piercy	78	76	154	Ryan Sullivan	81	82	163
*Gavin Hall	74	77	151	Eddie Pepperell	77	77	154	*Grayson Murray	83	81	164
*Max Homa	73	78	151	Jesse Smith	73	81	154	Louis Oosthuizen	75		WD
Nick Watney	73	78	151	Jay Don Blake	74	80	154	Robert Garrigus	80		WD
Bill Haas	77	74	151	Brandt Jobe	74	80	154				

Professionals not returning 72-hole scores received $2,000 each.

*Denotes amateur

113th U.S. OPEN Statistics

Hole	1	2	3	4	5	6	7	8	9	10	11	12	13	14	15	16	17	18	Total	
Par	4	5	3	5	4	4	4	4	3	4	4	4	3	4	4	4	3	4	70	
Justin Rose																				
Round 1	4	[6]	3	5	[5]	(3)	(3)	4	3	(3)	(3)	4	3	[5]	[5]	4	3	[5]	71	
Round 2	(3)	(4)	3	5	4	[5]	4	(3)	3	4	4	4	3	4	[5]	4	3	4	69	
Round 3	4	5	3	(4)	[5]	[5]	4	4	3	(3)	4	4	(2)	4	4	4	[4]	[5]	71	
Round 4	4	5	[4]	(4)	[5]	(3)	(3)	4	3	4	[5]	(3)	(2)	[5]	4	[5]	3	4	70	281
Jason Day																				
Round 1	(3)	[6]	3	5	[5]	4	4	4	(2)	(3)	4	(2)	4	(3)	[5]	[4]	[5]		70	
Round 2	4	5	[4]	5	4	[5]	4	[5]	[4]	4	4	(3)	3	4	[5]	(3)	3	[5]	74	
Round 3	4	5	3	(4)	[5]	[5]	(3)	4	3	(3)	4	4	(2)	4	4	4	(2)	[5]	68	
Round 4	4	5	3	(4)	[5]	4	4	(3)	3	(3)	[5]	4	3	[5]	4	4	3	[5]	71	283
Phil Mickelson																				
Round 1	(3)	5	3	5	4	4	(3)	4	(2)	4	[5]	4	(2)	4	4	4	3	4	67	
Round 2	[5]	5	3	5	4	4	4	4	3	4	4	[5]	[4]	4	4	4	3	(3)	72	
Round 3	4	5	[4]	5	[5]	4	4	4	3	(3)	(3)	4	3	4	4	4	(2)	[5]	70	
Round 4	4	5	[5]	(4)	[6]	4	4	4	3	(2)	4	4	[4]	4	[5]	4	3	[5]	74	283

○ Circled numbers represent birdies or eagles.   ☐ Squared numbers represent bogeys or worse.

Hole	Yards	Par	Eagles	Birdies	Pars	Bogeys	Double Bogeys	Higher	Average
1	350	4	1	81	308	58	8	1	3.987
2	556	5	3	96	266	71	15	6	5.042
3	256	3	0	27	266	151	13	0	3.328
4	628	5	0	54	279	99	17	8	5.230
5	504	4	0	12	169	220	51	4	4.706
6	487	4	0	23	235	171	26	1	4.445
7	360	4	0	62	300	80	10	4	4.110
8	359	4	2	83	287	77	6	1	4.011
9	236	3	0	23	273	129	28	3	3.375
OUT	3736	36	6	461	2383	1056	174	28	38.237
10	303	4	4	124	257	56	12	3	3.906
11	367	4	0	70	258	102	21	6	4.206
12	403	4	0	58	298	85	14	2	4.133
13	115	3	0	126	291	39	1	0	2.814
14	464	4	0	30	243	147	28	9	4.444
15	411	4	0	42	239	129	29	18	4.455
16	430	4	0	33	285	116	20	3	4.291
17	246	3	1	22	270	141	20	3	3.363
18	521	4	0	11	178	208	54	6	4.707
IN	3260	34	5	516	2319	1023	199	50	36.309
TOTAL	6996	70	11	977	4702	2079	373	78	74.546

113th U.S. OPEN Past Results

Date	Winner	Score	Runner-Up	Venue
1895	Horace Rawlins	173 - 36 holes	Willie Dunn	Newport G.C., Newport, R.I.
1896	James Foulis	152 - 36 holes	Horace Rawlins	Shinnecock Hills G.C., Southampton, N.Y.
1897	Joe Lloyd	162 - 36 holes	Willie Anderson	Chicago G.C., Wheaton, Ill.
1898	Fred Herd	328 - 72 holes	Alex Smith	Myopia Hunt Club, South Hamilton, Mass.
1899	Willie Smith	315	George Low, Val Fitzjohn, W.H. Way	Baltimore C.C., Baltimore, Md.
1900	Harry Vardon	313	J.H. Taylor	Chicago G.C., Wheaton, Ill.
1901	*Willie Anderson (85)	331	Alex Smith (86)	Myopia Hunt Club, South Hamilton, Mass.
1902	Laurence Auchterlonie	307	Stewart Gardner, Walter J. Travis	Garden City G.C., Garden City, N.Y.
1903	*Willie Anderson (82)	307	David Brown (84)	Baltusrol G.C., Springfield, N.J.
1904	Willie Anderson	303	Gilbert Nicholls	Glen View Club, Golf, Ill.
1905	Willie Anderson	314	Alex Smith	Myopia Hunt Club, South Hamilton, Mass.
1906	Alex Smith	295	Willie Smith	Onwentsia Club, Lake Forest, Ill.
1907	Alex Ross	302	Gilbert Nicholls	Philadelphia Cricket Club, Chestnut Hill, Pa.
1908	*Fred McLeod (77)	322	Willie Smith (83)	Myopia Hunt Club, South Hamilton, Mass.
1909	George Sargent	290	Tom McNamara	Englewood G.C., Englewood, N.J.
1910	*Alex Smith (71)	298	John J. McDermott (75), Macdonald Smith (77)	Philadelphia Cricket Club, Chestnut Hill, Pa.
1911	*John J. McDermott (80)	307	Michael J. Brady (82), George O. Simpson (85)	Chicago G.C., Wheaton, Ill.
1912	John J. McDermott	294	Tom McNamara	C.C. of Buffalo, Buffalo, N.Y.
1913	*Francis Ouimet (72)	304	Harry Vardon (77), Edward Ray (78)	The Country Club, Brookline, Mass.
1914	Walter Hagen	290	Charles Evans Jr.	Midlothian C.C., Blue Island, Ill.
1915	Jerome D. Travers	297	Tom McNamara	Baltusrol G.C., Springfield, N.J.
1916	Charles Evans Jr.	286	Jock Hutchison	Minikahda Club, Minneapolis, Minn.
1917-18	No Championships Played — World War I			
1919	*Walter Hagen (77)	301	Michael J. Brady (78)	Brae Burn C.C., West Newton, Mass.
1920	Edward Ray	295	Harry Vardon, Jack Burke Sr., Leo Diegel, Jock Hutchison	Inverness Club, Toledo, Ohio
1921	James M. Barnes	289	Walter Hagen, Fred McLeod	Columbia C.C., Chevy Chase, Md.
1922	Gene Sarazen	288	Robert T. Jones Jr., John L. Black	Skokie C.C., Glencoe, Ill.
1923	*Robert T. Jones Jr. (76)	296	Bobby Cruickshank (78)	Inwood C.C., Inwood, N.Y.
1924	Cyril Walker	297	Robert T. Jones Jr.	Oakland Hills C.C., Birmingham, Mich.
1925	*William Macfarlane (147)	291	Robert T. Jones Jr. (148)	Worcester C.C., Worcester, Mass.
1926	Robert T. Jones Jr.	293	Joe Turnesa	Scioto C.C., Columbus, Ohio
1927	*Tommy Armour (76)	301	Harry Cooper (79)	Oakmont C.C., Oakmont, Pa.
1928	*Johnny Farrell (143)	294	Robert T. Jones Jr. (144)	Olympia Fields C.C., Matteson, Ill.
1929	*Robert T. Jones Jr. (141)	294	Al Espinosa (164)	Winged Foot G.C., Mamaroneck, N.Y.
1930	Robert T. Jones Jr.	287	Macdonald Smith	Interlachen C.C., Minneapolis, Minn.
1931	*Billy Burke (149-148)	292	George Von Elm (149-149)	Inverness Club, Toledo, Ohio

Past Results

Date	Winner	Score	Runner-Up	Venue
1932	Gene Sarazen	286	Bobby Cruickshank, T. Philip Perkins	Fresh Meadow C.C., Flushing, N.Y.
1933	John Goodman	287	Ralph Guldahl	North Shore G.C., Glenview, Ill.
1934	Olin Dutra	293	Gene Sarazen	Merion Cricket Club, Ardmore, Pa.
1935	Sam Parks Jr.	299	Jimmy Thomson	Oakmont C.C., Oakmont, Pa.
1936	Tony Manero	282	Harry Cooper	Baltusrol G.C., Springfield, N.J.
1937	Ralph Guldahl	281	Sam Snead	Oakland Hills C.C., Birmingham, Mich.
1938	Ralph Guldahl	284	Dick Metz	Cherry Hills C.C., Englewood, Colo.
1939	*Byron Nelson (68-70)	284	Craig Wood (68-73), Denny Shute (76)	Philadelphia C.C., West Conshohocken, Pa.
1940	*Lawson Little (70)	287	Gene Sarazen (73)	Canterbury G.C., Cleveland, Ohio
1941	Craig Wood	284	Denny Shute	Colonial C.C., Fort Worth, Texas
1942-45	No Championships Played — World War II			
1946	*Lloyd Mangrum (72-72)	284	Byron Nelson (72-73), Victor Ghezzi (72-73)	Canterbury G.C., Cleveland, Ohio
1947	*Lew Worsham (69)	282	Sam Snead (70)	St. Louis C.C., Clayton, Mo.
1948	Ben Hogan	276	Jimmy Demaret	Riviera C.C., Los Angeles, Calif.
1949	Cary Middlecoff	286	Sam Snead, Clayton Heafner	Medinah C.C., Medinah, Ill.
1950	*Ben Hogan (69)	287	Lloyd Mangrum (73), George Fazio (75)	Merion G.C., Ardmore, Pa.
1951	Ben Hogan	287	Clayton Heafner	Oakland Hills C.C., Birmingham, Mich.
1952	Julius Boros	281	Ed Oliver	Northwood Club, Dallas, Texas
1953	Ben Hogan	283	Sam Snead	Oakmont C.C., Oakmont, Pa.
1954	Ed Furgol	284	Gene Littler	Baltusrol G.C., Springfield, N.J.
1955	*Jack Fleck (69)	287	Ben Hogan (72)	The Olympic Club, San Francisco, Calif.
1956	Cary Middlecoff	281	Julius Boros, Ben Hogan	Oak Hill C.C., Rochester, N.Y.
1957	*Dick Mayer (72)	282	Cary Middlecoff (79)	Inverness Club, Toledo, Ohio
1958	Tommy Bolt	283	Gary Player	Southern Hills C.C., Tulsa, Okla.
1959	Billy Casper	282	Bob Rosburg	Winged Foot G.C., Mamaroneck, N.Y.
1960	Arnold Palmer	280	Jack Nicklaus	Cherry Hills C.C., Englewood, Colo.
1961	Gene Littler	281	Doug Sanders, Bob Goalby	Oakland Hills C.C., Birmingham, Mich.
1962	*Jack Nicklaus (71)	283	Arnold Palmer (74)	Oakmont C.C., Oakmont, Pa.
1963	*Julius Boros (70)	293	Jacky Cupit (73), Arnold Palmer (76)	The Country Club, Brookline, Mass.
1964	Ken Venturi	278	Tommy Jacobs	Congressional C.C., Bethesda, Md.
1965	*Gary Player (71)	282	Kel Nagle (74)	Bellerive C.C., St. Louis, Mo.
1966	*Billy Casper (69)	278	Arnold Palmer (73)	The Olympic Club, San Francisco, Calif.
1967	Jack Nicklaus	275	Arnold Palmer	Baltusrol G.C., Springfield, N.J.
1968	Lee Trevino	275	Jack Nicklaus	Oak Hill C.C., Rochester, N.Y.
1969	Orville Moody	281	Deane Beman, Al Geiberger, Bob Rosburg	Champions G.C., Houston, Texas
1970	Tony Jacklin	281	Dave Hill	Hazeltine National G.C., Chaska, Minn.
1971	*Lee Trevino (68)	280	Jack Nicklaus (71)	Merion G.C., Ardmore, Pa.
1972	Jack Nicklaus	290	Bruce Crampton	Pebble Beach G.L., Pebble Beach, Calif.
1973	Johnny Miller	279	John Schlee	Oakmont C.C., Oakmont, Pa.
1974	Hale Irwin	287	Forrest Fezler	Winged Foot G.C., Mamaroneck, N.Y.
1975	*Lou Graham (71)	287	John Mahaffey (73)	Medinah C.C., Medinah, Ill.
1976	Jerry Pate	277	Tom Weiskopf, Al Geiberger	Atlanta Athletic Club, Duluth, Ga.

Date	Winner	Score	Runner-Up	Venue
1977	Hubert Green	278	Lou Graham	Southern Hills C.C., Tulsa, Okla.
1978	Andy North	285	J.C. Snead, Dave Stockton	Cherry Hills C.C., Englewood, Colo.
1979	Hale Irwin	284	Gary Player, Jerry Pate	Inverness Club, Toledo, Ohio
1980	Jack Nicklaus	272	Isao Aoki	Baltusrol G.C., Springfield, N.J.
1981	David Graham	273	Bill Rogers, George Burns	Merion G.C., Ardmore, Pa.
1982	Tom Watson	282	Jack Nicklaus	Pebble Beach G.L., Pebble Beach, Calif.
1983	Larry Nelson	280	Tom Watson	Oakmont C.C., Oakmont, Pa.
1984	*Fuzzy Zoeller (67)	276	Greg Norman (75)	Winged Foot G.C., Mamaroneck, N.Y.
1985	Andy North	279	Denis Watson, Dave Barr, Tze-Chung Chen	Oakland Hills C.C., Birmingham, Mich.
1986	Raymond Floyd	279	Lanny Wadkins, Chip Beck	Shinnecock Hills G.C., Southampton, N.Y.
1987	Scott Simpson	277	Tom Watson	The Olympic Club, San Francisco, Calif.
1988	*Curtis Strange (71)	278	Nick Faldo (75)	The Country Club, Brookline, Mass.
1989	Curtis Strange	278	Ian Woosnam, Chip Beck, Mark McCumber	Oak Hill C.C., Rochester, N.Y.
1990	*Hale Irwin (74+3)	280	Mike Donald (74+4)	Medinah C.C., Medinah, Ill.
1991	*Payne Stewart (75)	282	Scott Simpson (77)	Hazeltine National G.C., Chaska, Minn.
1992	Tom Kite	285	Jeff Sluman	Pebble Beach G.L., Pebble Beach, Calif.
1993	Lee Janzen	272	Payne Stewart	Baltusrol G.C., Springfield, N.J.
1994	*Ernie Els (74+4+4)	279	Loren Roberts (74+4+5), Colin Montgomerie (78)	Oakmont C.C., Oakmont, Pa.
1995	Corey Pavin	280	Greg Norman	Shinnecock Hills G.C., Southampton, N.Y.
1996	Steve Jones	278	Tom Lehman, Davis Love III	Oakland Hills C.C., Bloomfield Hills, Mich.
1997	Ernie Els	276	Colin Montgomerie	Congressional C.C., Bethesda, Md.
1998	Lee Janzen	280	Payne Stewart	The Olympic Club, San Francisco, Calif.
1999	Payne Stewart	279	Phil Mickelson	Pinehurst R&CC, Village of Pinehurst, N.C.
2000	Tiger Woods	272	Ernie Els, Miguel Angel Jimenez	Pebble Beach G.L., Pebble Beach, Calif.
2001	*Retief Goosen (70)	276	Mark Brooks (72)	Southern Hills C.C., Tulsa, Okla.
2002	Tiger Woods	277	Phil Mickelson	Bethpage State Park, Farmingdale, N.Y.
2003	Jim Furyk	272	Stephen Leaney	Olympia Fields C.C., Olympia Fields, Ill.
2004	Retief Goosen	276	Phil Mickelson	Shinnecock Hills G.C., Southampton, N.Y.
2005	Michael Campbell	280	Tiger Woods	Pinehurst Resort, Village of Pinehurst, N.C.
2006	Geoff Ogilvy	285	Jim Furyk, Colin Montgomerie, Phil Mickelson	Winged Foot G.C., Mamaroneck, N.Y.
2007	Angel Cabrera	285	Jim Furyk, Tiger Woods	Oakmont C.C., Oakmont, Pa.
2008	*Tiger Woods (71+4)	283	Rocco Mediate (71+5)	Torrey Pines G.C., San Diego, Calif.
2009	Lucas Glover	276	Phil Mickelson, David Duval, Ricky Barnes	Bethpage State Park, Farmingdale, N.Y.
2010	Graeme McDowell	284	Gregory Havret	Pebble Beach G.L., Pebble Beach, Calif.
2011	Rory McIlroy	268	Jason Day	Congressional C.C., Bethesda, Md.
2012	Webb Simpson	281	Michael Thompson, Graeme McDowell	The Olympic Club, San Francisco, Calif.
2013	Justin Rose	281	Jason Day, Phil Mickelson	Merion G.C., Ardmore, Pa.

*Winner in playoff; figures in parentheses indicate scores

113th U.S. OPEN Championship Records

Oldest champion (years/months/days)
45/0/15 — Hale Irwin (1990)

Youngest champion
19/10/14 — John J. McDermott (1911)

Most victories
4 — Willie Anderson (1901, '03, '04, '05)
4 — Robert T. Jones Jr. (1923, '26, '29, '30)
4 — Ben Hogan (1948, '50, '51, '53)
4 — Jack Nicklaus (1962, '67, '72, '80)
3 — Hale Irwin (1974, '79, '90), Tiger Woods (2000, '02, '08)
2 — by 15 players: Alex Smith (1906, '10), John J. McDermott (1911, '12), Walter Hagen (1914, '19), Gene Sarazen (1922, '32), Ralph Guldahl (1937, '38), Cary Middlecoff (1949, '56), Julius Boros (1952, '63), Billy Casper (1959, '66), Lee Trevino (1968, '71), Andy North (1978, '85), Curtis Strange (1988, '89), Payne Stewart (1991, '99), Lee Janzen (1993, '98), Ernie Els (1994, '97), and Retief Goosen (2001, '04)

Consecutive victories
3 — Willie Anderson (1903, '04, '05)
2 — John J. McDermott (1911, '12)
2 — Robert T. Jones Jr. (1929, '30)
2 — Ralph Guldahl (1937, '38)
2 — Ben Hogan (1950, '51)
2 — Curtis Strange (1988, '89)

Most times runner-up
6 — Phil Mickelson
4 — Robert T. Jones Jr.
4 — Sam Snead
4 — Jack Nicklaus
4 — Arnold Palmer

Longest course
7,643 yards — Torrey Pines G.C. (South Course), San Diego, Calif. (2008)

Shortest course
Since World War II
6,528 yards — Merion G.C. (East Course), Ardmore, Pa. (1971, '81)

Most often host club of U.S. Open
8 — Oakmont (Pa.) C.C. (1927, '35, '53, '62, '73, '83, '94, 2007)
7 — Baltusrol G.C., Springfield, N.J. (1903, '15, '36, '54, '67, '80, '93)

Largest entry
9,860 (2013)

Smallest entry
11 (1895)

Lowest score, 72 holes
268 — Rory McIlroy (65-66-68-69), at Congressional C.C., Bethesda, Md. (2011)

Lowest score, first 54 holes
199 — Rory McIlroy (65-66-68), at Congressional C.C., Bethesda, Md. (2011)

Lowest score, last 54 holes
203 — Loren Roberts (69-64-70), at Oakmont (Pa.) C.C. (1994)
203 — Rory McIlroy (66-68-69), at Congressional C.C., Bethesda, Md. (2011)

Lowest score, first 36 holes
131 — Rory McIlroy (65-66), at Congressional C.C., Bethesda, Md. (2011)

Lowest score, last 36 holes
132 — Larry Nelson (65-67), at Oakmont (Pa.) C.C. (1983)

Lowest score, 9 holes
29 — Neal Lancaster (second nine, final round), at Shinnecock Hills G.C., Southampton, N.Y. (1995)
29 — Neal Lancaster (second nine, second round), at Oakland Hills C.C. (South Course), Bloomfield Hills, Mich. (1996)
29 — Vijay Singh (second nine, second round), at Olympia Fields (Ill.) C.C. (North Course) (2003)

Lowest score, 18 holes
63 — Johnny Miller, final round at Oakmont (Pa.) C.C. (1973)
63 — Jack Nicklaus, first round at Baltusrol G.C. (Lower Course), Springfield, N.J. (1980)
63 — Tom Weiskopf, first round at Baltusrol G.C. (Lower Course), Springfield, N.J. (1980)
63 — Vijay Singh, second round at Olympia Fields (Ill.) C.C. (North Course) (2003)

Largest winning margin
15 — Tiger Woods (272), at Pebble Beach (Calif.) G.L. (2000)

Highest winning score
Since World War II
293 — Julius Boros, at The Country Club (Championship Course), Brookline, Mass. (1963) (won in playoff)

Best first round by champion
63 — Jack Nicklaus, at Baltusrol G.C. (Lower Course), Springfield, N.J. (1980)

Best final round by champion
63 — Johnny Miller, at Oakmont (Pa.) C.C. (1973)

Worst first round by champion
Since World War II
76 — Ben Hogan, at Oakland Hills C.C. (South Course), Birmingham, Mich. (1951)
76 — Jack Fleck, at The Olympic Club (Lake Course), San Francisco, Calif. (1955)

Worst final round by champion
  Since World War II
  75 — Cary Middlecoff, at Medinah (Ill.) C.C. (No. 3 Course) (1949)
  75 — Hale Irwin, at Inverness Club, Toledo, Ohio (1979)
Lowest score to lead field, 18 holes
  63 — Jack Nicklaus and Tom Weiskopf, at Baltusrol G.C. (Lower Course), Springfield, N.J. (1980)
Lowest score to lead field, 36 holes
  131 — Rory McIlroy (65-66), at Congressional C.C., Bethesda, Md. (2011)
Lowest score to lead field, 54 holes
  199 — Rory McIlroy (65-66-68), at Congressional C.C., Bethesda, Md. (2011)
Highest score to lead field, 18 holes
  Since World War II
  71 — Sam Snead, at Oakland Hills C.C. (South Course), Birmingham, Mich. (1951)
  71 — Tommy Bolt, Julius Boros and Dick Metz, at Southern Hills C.C., Tulsa, Okla. (1958)
  71 — Tony Jacklin, at Hazeltine National G.C., Chaska, Minn. (1970)
  71 — Orville Moody, Jack Nicklaus, Chi Chi Rodriguez, Mason Rudolph, Tom Shaw and Kermit Zarley, at Pebble Beach (Calif.) G.L. (1972)
Highest score to lead field, 36 holes
  Since World War II
  144 — Bobby Locke (73-71), at Oakland Hills C.C. (South Course), Birmingham, Mich. (1951)
  144 — Tommy Bolt (67-77) and E. Harvie Ward (74-70), at The Olympic Club (Lake Course), San Francisco, Calif. (1955)
  144 — Homero Blancas (74-70), Bruce Crampton (74-70), Jack Nicklaus (71-73), Cesar Sanudo (72-72), Lanny Wadkins (76-68) and Kermit Zarley (71-73), at Pebble Beach (Calif.) G.L. (1972)
Highest score to lead field, 54 holes
  Since World War II
  218 — Bobby Locke (73-71-74), at Oakland Hills C.C. (South Course), Birmingham, Mich. (1951)
  218 — Jacky Cupit (70-72-76), at The Country Club (Championship Course), Brookline, Mass. (1963)
Lowest 36-hole cut
  143 — at Olympia Fields (Ill.) C.C. (North Course) (2003)
Highest 36-hole cut
  155 — at The Olympic Club (Lake Course), San Francisco, Calif. (1955)
Most players to tie for lead, 36 holes
  6 — at Pebble Beach (Calif.) G.L. (1972)
Most players to tie for lead, 54 holes
  4 — at Oakmont (Pa.) C.C. (1973)

Most sub-par rounds, championship
  124 — at Medinah (Ill.) C.C. (No. 3 Course) (1990)
Most sub-par 72-hole totals, championship
  28 — at Medinah (Ill.) C.C. (No. 3 Course) (1990)
Most sub-par scores, first round
  39 — at Medinah (Ill.) C.C. (No. 3 Course) (1990)
Most sub-par scores, second round
  47 — at Medinah (Ill.) C.C. (No. 3 Course) (1990)
Most sub-par scores, third round
  26 — at Congressional C.C., Bethesda, Md. (2011)
Most sub-par scores, fourth round
  32 — at Congressional C.C., Bethesda, Md. (2011)
Most sub-par rounds by one player in one championship
  4 — Sam Snead (includes playoff), at St. Louis (Mo.) C.C. (1947)
  4 — Billy Casper, at The Olympic Club (Lake Course), San Francisco, Calif. (1966)
  4 — Lee Trevino, at Oak Hill C.C. (East Course), Rochester, N.Y. (1968)
  4 — Tony Jacklin, at Hazeltine National G.C., Chaska, Minn. (1970)
  4 — Lee Janzen, at Baltusrol G.C. (Lower Course), Springfield, N.J. (1993)
  4 — Curtis Strange, at Oakmont (Pa.) C.C. (1994)
  4 — Rory McIlroy, at Congressional C.C., Bethesda, Md. (2011)
  4 — Robert Garrigus, at Congressional C.C., Bethesda, Md. (2011)
Highest score, one hole
  19 — Ray Ainsley, at the 16th (par 4) at Cherry Hills C.C., Englewood, Colo. (1938)
Most consecutive birdies
  6 — George Burns (holes 2–7), at Pebble Beach (Calif.) G.L. (1972)
  6 — Andy Dillard (holes 1–6), at Pebble Beach (Calif.) G.L. (1992)
Most consecutive 3s
  8 — Hubert Green (holes 9–16), at Baltusrol G.C. (Lower Course), Springfield, N.J. (1980)
  7 — Hubert Green (holes 10–16), at Southern Hills C.C., Tulsa, Okla. (1977)
  7 — Peter Jacobsen (holes 1–7), at The Country Club (Championship Course), Brookline, Mass. (1988)
Most consecutive U.S. Opens started
  44 — Jack Nicklaus (1957-2000)
Most U.S. Opens completed 72 holes
  35 — Jack Nicklaus
Most consecutive U.S. Opens completed 72 holes
  22 — Walter Hagen (1913-36; no championships 1917-18)
  22 — Gene Sarazen (1920-41)
  22 — Gary Player (1958-79)

Veteran golf writer and editor **David Shedloski** has been covering the game since 1986 and contributes to a number of golf-based websites and publications, including usopen.com and usga.org. He serves as editorial director of *Memorial Magazine* and is a contributing writer to *Golf World* magazine and GolfDigest.com. In addition, he has authored, co-authored or contributed to many books, including the *U.S. Open Annual* since 2008.

The members of the **USGA Team** who contributed to this book are: Photographers: USGA Manager of Creative Services **John Mummert, Darren Carroll, Michael Cohen, Steve Gibbons, Jonathan Kolbe, Joel Kowsky, Hunter Martin**; Photo Editors: **Chris Keane, Porter Binks, Jessica Foster, Mike Zacchino**; Assistant Photo Editors: **Nicole Ciaramella, Matt Godfrey**; Copyeditor: **Ron Driscoll**.

Par and Yardage

Hole	Par	Yardage	Hole	Par	Yardage
1	4	350	10	4	303
2	5	556	11	4	367
3	3	256	12	4	403
4	5	628	13	3	115
5	4	504	14	4	464
6	4	487	15	4	411
7	4	360	16	4	430
8	4	359	17	3	246
9	3	236	18	4	521
	36	3,736		34	3,260
			TOTAL	70	6,996